HONG KONG
Borrowed Place—Borrowed Time

RICHARD HUGHES

Hong Kong

Borrowed Place—
Borrowed Time

FREDERICK A. PRAEGER, *Publishers*

New York • Washington • London

FREDERICK A. PRAEGER, PUBLISHERS
111 Fourth Avenue, New York, N.Y. 10003, U.S.A.
5, Cromwell Place, London S.W.7, England

Published in the United States of America in 1968
by Frederick A. Praeger, Inc., Publishers

Second printing, 1968

Library of Congress Catalog Card Number: 68-12379

Printed in the United States of America

ACKNOWLEDGEMENT

Acknowledgement is made, with respect and affection, to Han Suyin for the sub-title of this book, Borrowed Place — Borrowed Time, which is from her eloquent *apologia* of Hong Kong's survival, resilience and destiny in an article in *Life* (1959), entitled 'Hong Kong's Ten-Year Miracle':

Squeezed between giant antagonists crunching huge bones of contention, Hong Kong has achieved within its own narrow territories a co-existence which is baffling, infuriating, incomprehensible, and works splendidly—on borrowed time in a borrowed place.

Han Suyin herself, in this story, attributes the phrase to a Hong Kong resident named Tom Wu, whom she described as a former Shanghai businessman, 'a gourmet and something of a poet', who had quit Shanghai when the Communists arrived: 'Prosperous but precarious, energetic on borrowed time in a borrowed place, that is Hong Kong'.

So this acknowledgement goes to Tom Wu as well as to Han Suyin.

Contents

Hong Kong Today

BORROWED PLACE — BORROWED TIME

A borrowed place living on borrowed time, Hong Kong is an
impudent capitalist survival on China's communist *derriere*,
an anachronistic mixture of British colonialism and the Chinese
way of life, a jumble of millionaires' mansions and horrible
slums, a teeming mass of hard-working humans, a well-ordered
autocracy.

It was founded on contraband and conquest, it is insufficient
in food and water, it lacks coal, oil and all natural resources
save granite, sand, fish and *homo sapiens*. It is a rambunctious,
freebooting colony, naked and unashamed, devoid of self-pity,
regrets or fear of the future.

Life, as in most of Asia, is hard and cruel for many. There
are gross extremes of wealth and poverty reminiscent of Shanghai
in the thirties and forties. The hanging gardens and golden
roofs of terraced villas on The Peak overlook the diseased scabs
of squatters' huts corroding distant hillsides, the fleets of junks
and sampans that are the floating homes of 100,000 people, and
the huddled packed tenements, where another 80,000 subsist
illegally on the rooftops, and which succumb so often to typhoon
and fire or collapse from old age.

The city-port slices down mountains and fills in waterfront shallows to make more elbow-room for its four million residents, expanding factories and ever-rising skyscrapers. It is the only human habitation in the world that knows when it will die — 1997, when the lease on the ceded New Territories expires and nine-tenths of the colony must be handed back to China. But no one broods over this deadline — which can be advanced whenever Peking has a change of policy and a change of mind. No one goes hungry. There is no feeling of despair or hope-lessness. Fratricidal enemies of China's bitter civil war live together — or *have* lived together — in harmony under a foreign flag. 1997 is still three enigmatic decades distant. Borrowed time is as good as any.

So Hong Kong, politically neuter, dedicated to the *laisser-faire* economics of the nineteenth century and employing the industrial technique of the twentieth century, offers offence to no one and seeks help from no one, asks only to be allowed to work and live.

In today's world, Hong Kong is an improbability — one had almost said an impossibility. But it works. Or rather, it *has* worked, but only because it has been accepted by its giant Communist neighbour as an integral part of China under the rule of a foreign, capitalist government. Peking could crush it by fomenting anarchy and disorder and then sending 'protective' troops across the frontier at the risk of a world war. Peking could strangle it by cutting off trade and supplies. Peking could administer the lingering 'death of a thousand cuts' by simply scaring away capital investment.

Optimists say that Peking is too smart to do any of these things because Hong Kong is too useful, convenient and profitable for China. This hope, alas, derives piously from the argument that sanity and logic prevail in China today.

Neither efficiency nor harmony protects a colony in the twentieth century. Singapore is now a city-republic. Shanghai has been restored to the bosom of the Chinese· people — or rulers. The Dutch and the French have fled Asia. Macao, Hong Kong's neighbour on the South China Coasts, has now been contemptuously denied even the empty pretence of Portuguese authority to which it had clung humbly since the 'liberation' of China. Even the pacifist Nehru was forced by public opinion to take up the gun and take over Goa.

The Union Jack flying over Hong Kong, and evoking memories of opium wars and the humiliation of the Emperor by the western barbarians, is more an imperialist affront to Chinese nationalist pride than a capitalist affront to Communist dogma. Chinese Communism, after all, is resurgent nationalist pride first, and Maoist-Marxist ideology second. Chiang Kai-shek's Nationalists denounced Hong Kong in the past as fiercely as Mao's Communists have done since.

There has been recent democratic lobbying, in Rotarian depth, to drop the dirty word 'colony' and have the place rechristened 'free city state' or 'free port state.' But no one cares very much. A colony by any other name would only smell fishier.

So can the Hong Kong miracle expect to survive until 1997? The answer will be found not in Hong Kong but in China. Probably Peking itself at the moment has no idea.

There is no democratic nonsense in Hong Kong. There is, to date, no political sense or instinct. There are no serious demands for a vote, for a wider franchise, or for self-government — which last dream would have the Communist and Nationalist factions at each other's throat, and which Peking, however expediently tolerant of a colony, could not possibly accept. The Union Jack is bad enough, but an independent Chinese government on Chinese soil would be unthinkable.

The 30,000 British and other foreign devils in Hong Kong, like the *taipans* ('Great Managers') in 'pre-liberation' Shanghai, have come to make a living, but not a home, in Hong Kong. The local Chinese, who can elect to move to any other part of Greater China, know that, whoever acts as local boss, Hong

Kong is, and remains, Chinese.   There is work and profit today. There will be work, and there may be profit, tomorrow — if tomorrow is allowed to come.   That is Hong Kong's credo.

THE PLACE AND THE PEOPLE

As with any port-city, it is best to arrive in Hong Kong by sea. Unlike Shanghai, whose incongruous Bund skyline looms on the horizon across the mudflats an hour before your ship completes the winding passage up the Whangpoo, Hong Kong's Manhattan-like skyscrapers and crowded blue-and-silver harbour burst like a bombshell mirage on the visitor.   The ship threads through deserted sugar-loaf islands — some Communist, some part of the colony — and enters the narrow Lyeyemun Pass to hit Hong Kong slap on the nose.   It is one of the world's most dramatic landfalls and one of the world's most spectacular harbours.

I have arrived at Shanghai twice by ship — before and after 'liberation' — and at Hong Kong twice by ship.   My nostrils are not over-sensitive, but on each occasion, at each port, at different times of the year, I have shared with fellow passengers immediate identification of a faint smell of flowers on the wings of the wind from Hong Kong, and a strong smell of burned sugar — that's the closest I can get—on the winds from Shanghai. There are plenty of flowers at Hong Kong, but don't ask me where the burned sugar is at Shanghai.

Hong Kong is largely sand and rock.   But it is no Gibraltar.   Hong Kong proper is a beautiful, mountainous, tropical island, ten miles long and about thirty square miles in area. You can drive around it on excellent roads, with magnificent seascapes, in about an hour.   Victoria, the central area, on the lower slopes of the 1,800-foot Peak, is the capital, but no one uses that name.   Hong Kong is 'the island' or 'Hong Kong side'.

Kowloon, the colony's toehold on the mainland, is only

$3\frac{1}{4}$ square miles in area. It was grabbed from the Chinese in 1861, eighteen years after Hong Kong island was similarly grabbed, so that the British could control the harbour which put Hong Kong on the map. The ferries make the crossing in about five minutes. Like the slums of Hong Kong island, Kowloon is a labyrinth of jam-packed, laundry-hung tenements, shops, factories and skyscrapers, bisected by a noble thoroughfare lined with banyan trees which is known as Nathan Road.

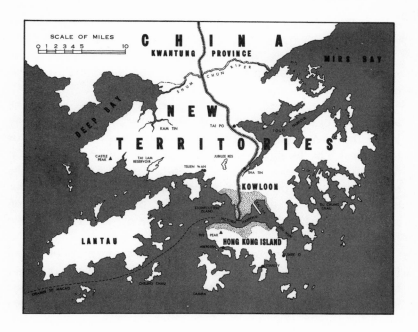

On the northern side of Boundary Street, where the colony technically ends, are, first, the huge spreading blocks of resettlement housing and Kaitak airport (stretching into the sea, because there is no room on shore), and then the mountains and the rolling Chinese countryside and farmlands of the New Territories. This is an area of 355 square miles and ends at the guarded, seventeen-mile, barbed-fence frontier of China. The railway journey from Kowloon to the border takes just one hour by Australian-built diesel locomotive.

The colony also includes nearly two hundred islands, mostly unsettled and barren. One, Lan Tao, is nearly double the size of Hong Kong, but is sparsely settled, rough and undeveloped, and probably looks today something like Hong Kong did before the British came in 1843. All told, in real estate and 'British waters', the colony is roughly forty miles wide and thirty miles deep. It is virtually surrounded by Chinese Communist islands with watchful garrisons.

Fifty miles away, on the western hook of the Pearl River estuary leading to Canton, is Macao, the ancient Portuguese outpost, of which more anon.

There is no agreement on whether Hong Kong should be spelt as one or two words. The Government seems to favour Hong Kong, but many government departments lump the two words together. The Hongkong and Shanghai Banking Corporation makes the best — or worst — of both worlds by spelling the name both ways on the same official cheque-forms. Chinese names are always difficult. Even the purists who insist on spelling Hong Kong in two words lump Kow and Loon ('Nine Dragons') together.

Scholars also argue about the English meaning of Hong Kong. Most agree that the operative word is 'Fragrant', but there is dispute about whether the other word should be 'Harbour' or 'Channel' or 'Waters' or 'Springs'. A dogged minority insists that the real meaning is 'Incense Harbour', that *heung* in Heung Kong (the original name of the fishing village now known as Aberdeen on Hong Kong island) referred to 'the maiden incense' or perfumed tree sap once produced and exported there. But the argument becomes esoteric and marginal.

The natives of Hong Kong tend to be friendly, interested in trade, and peaceful — except when a minority becomes

politically demented, or when from time to time they get up to
public commotion and rioting, in which a basic xenophobia is
immediately detectable. They are hard working and seldom
drink to excess. But they are crazy gamblers, and heroin
addiction has become a major problem. They like noise and
colour and eat in public with the same gay and infectious uproar
as the Italians. No foreigner who has been in a crowd on a
Hong Kong ferry or tried to get on a Hong Kong bus at a peak
hour can understand why anyone ever called the Chinese impassive. The women, all agree, are comely.

The population is a race of refugees. Of every thirty adults
in crowded streets or stores or parks or factories, twenty are
refugees. Some have fared better than others, but they all
came of their own choice and they prefer to stay. No one
need go hungry, there are few beggars — and these need not
beg — and even the worst poverty is better than slum conditions
in Djakarta or India.

They come from all parts of China, with provincial likes
and dislikes, regional prejudices and rivalries, but essential
unifying Chineseness. The husky expatriate from Peking and
the north, who prefers wheat to rice, scorns the uncouth speech,
barbarous habits and dainty food of the sharp, quick Cantonese,
who in turn sniffs at both the 'Peking clerk' and the 'Shanghai
crook'. The tough Shanghai cosmopolitan, who brought so
much capital into Hong Kong after the Communists took over,
regards the man from Peking as a provincial, and the man from
Canton as at best a shifty fellow and at worst a scoundrel. The
Hakka peasant in the New Territories knows that real happiness
comes only from the land; the Hoklo fisherman knows the same
thing about the sea.

Yet all contrive to get along well enough in pragmatic
acceptance of a common Hong Kong life and fate. Personal
envy is not a Chinese weakness. Indeed, in moments of im-
personal discussion, they use unconsciously the all-embracing
personal 'we' when referring to Hong Kong and its people. So

do British officials.

Because of the circumstances of their original exodus from China after the arrival of the Communists, most of Hong Kong's Chinese — who comprise 98 percent of the colony's four millions — are anti-Communist or, more correctly, non-Communist. But a new, restless and discontented generation is growing up, whose non-ideological aspirations for a better job and a better home are one of Hong Kong's imponderables. The essential point is that they are all Chinese. And being Chinese, none of them — coolie or banker, merchant or trader, new or old generation, Nationalist or Communist — ever doubts that, man for man, they are naturally superior to the Westerner.

The Chinese are more interested in superstition than religion and in devils than God, but there is said to have been a revival of Buddhism among anti-Communists in recent years, and there is no shortage of quiet temples and joss-houses in the traffic-packed streets and stairwayed back-alleys.

The foreign devils have brought their own churches and clubs to Hong Kong, live largely their own lives, and know only a limited section of well-to-do Chinese whose business interests and social habits cross theirs. The snobs and segregationists in the colony are seldom the red-faced, pink-ginned Old Hands. The worst offenders are young clerks and half-assed white-collar ex-suburbanites with prissy wives, who suddenly find themselves on a first foreign assignment with good quarters — and a servant or two, to boot.

In recent years, racial barriers — hypocritically claimed to be non-existent — have been lowered at some clubs. But exclusion, disguised or open, never worried the top-brass Chinese, who have their own subtler and stronger snobberies, and who practise their own anti-barbarian segregation in their own clubs. And such exclusion has of course no meaning or interest for the great mass of the Chinese, who would guffaw and spit at the idea of joining a club whether it was British or Chinese.

There is enough wild life in the colony's unsettled and wooded heights — to say nothing of wretched mongrels running loose and puppies being fattened for a Cantonese banquet delicacy — to keep a very British Society for the Prevention of Cruelty to Animals alert, active and anxious. There are barking deer and scaly ant-eaters and ferret badgers and civets and porcupines, eight species of rats and mice, two of shrews, and at least ten species of bats, including the dog-faced fruit bat, which for some doubtless good reason insists on nesting only under Chinese fanpalms. The wild boar has been killed off, like the crab-eating mongoose, the rhesus monkey and the Communist's faithful friend the dhole — a red, and presumably therefore not a running, dog.

There are also enough birds to keep a very British Society of Bird Watchers expectant, binoculared and exultant. There are grebes and herons, shrikes and drongos, babblers and kingfishers, hawks and eagles, crakes and rails, owls and cockatoos (also a francolin whose sharp prolonged call is claimed by the imaginative to sound like, 'Come to The Peak, ha, ha!').

But there are no seagulls in the harbour: Hong Kong throws away nothing that can be eaten or sold.

WHAT MAKES HONG KONG RUN?

Power in Hong Kong, it has been said, resides in the Jockey Club, Jardine and Matheson, the Hong Kong and Shanghai Bank, and the Governor — in that order. There is more than a grain of truth in the observation. A vulnerable but durable colony, with a sturdy, old-fashioned, free trade philosophy, and uncompromising dedication to the principles of Adam Smith, requires an Establishment whose order of precedence expediently unites Big Business with Government. 'Those who are not on our side are against us,' as Chairman Mao has pointed out.

The Hong Kong formula for success is just as simple and straightforward: low taxes, no controls, quick profits, hard work, *laisser - faire.*

The colony refuses to be bothered with official estimates of national income. Nor does it worry about balance of payments. It rolls coolly with the blows as export earnings fluctuate, taking body punishment without complaint, and accepting any lead on points at the end of a round without elation. A reliable unofficial estimate puts the national income at over HK$8,000 million, and reckons the annual growth rate at eight percent.

Wages, costs and depreciation reflect the export market. It is a free port, and its economy is based on exports rather than on the domestic market. Virtually all capital expenditure comes out of current revenue. The cake is just so big, and the slices are quickly grabbed and gobbled — like the crumbs which fall from the table for social welfare and higher living standards.

Long-term borrowing is difficult: how many investors who can get — or have been getting — their money back in five to seven years from *laisser-faire* operations can be expected to let the Government have it for twenty years? More public building — schools and houses — means less private building, the Establishment argues. Higher taxes, like controls, will frighten away the flood of investment money which keeps the workers employed, boosts exports, and makes Hong Kong run.

Anyway, living standards and wages are rising — and so are living costs and expenses. So why monkey around with a winning combination? Perhaps it will be practicable to juggle the budget so that, without a harmful diversion of capital, social welfare expenditure can be raised from the current pettifogging 1.1 percent allowance. Taxation has remained pegged at a maximum of 12½ percent; an instructive index of progress is that, at that gentle fixed rate, the Government's tax receipts have been averaging an increase of fifteen percent over recent years. But Hong Kong, the pessimists say, must become the victim of its own growing affluence, and, as it develops its own domestic market, rising wages must affect export costs.

Since the May 1967 riots revealed the new latent threat of

any wildcat strike to the colony's law and order and even survival, labour and management have been urged to get together
as closely as government and management have got together.
The aspiration is as admirable as the poet Li Po's attempt to
embrace the image of the full moon in the lotus pond, and the
chances of success at the present time are about as slender.
But it is an essential and basic line of endeavour which must be
patiently explored.

Government and industry continue to work, consult and
agree with that close Hong Kong harmony at the top which
still makes it difficult to say which of the two initiates policy.
And despite, or perhaps because of, *laisser-faire,* the Government finds itself getting into many capital investment projects
such as factory building and development of new towns in the
rural New Territories.

'Hong Kong can prosper only so long as it remains economically free,' as one Government chief has put it, adding hastily,
'but of course the economy needs guidance.'

Hong Kong's hard-won success has of course raised against
its exports the very trade barriers which the colony itself disdains.
The Government remains steadfast to free trade policies and,
without exactly turning the other cheek, rejects retaliation as
firmly as it refuses subsidies to industry.   Textile quotas and
other impediments have served only to spur the colony's enterprise, and to encourage diversification of industry.   Just as
toys and artificial flowers followed textiles, so now are plastics
and electronics being developed.

Because of the alarums and excursions across the border,
Chinese entrepreneurs in Hong Kong develop the *sang-froid*
of Italian peasants living on the slopes of Vesuvius.   In the
colony, they say that an 'economic setback' is 'an opportunity
for adjustment', and that a 'recession' means 'a profit of only
one hundred percent'.

*   *   *

All land in Hong Kong is the property of the British Crown. Leases are sold to the highest bidder at public auction, whether the land is intended for residential, commercial or industrial purposes. Back in the old carefree days, Crown leases were granted for 75, 99 or 999 years. Nowadays the lease runs for a conservative 75 years, renewable hopefully for another 75 years. In the New Territories, a realistic amendment now limits a lease to 99 years from July 1, 1898, *less three days,* so terminating the contract three days before the expiration of the 99-year lease from China. It is a precise clause: three days, one supposes, is an appropriate interval for packing up and moving out before the landlords move in.

Land for public utilities, schools, clinics, special housing and approved charitable purposes is granted by private charter.

The magnificent deep-water port which put Hong Kong on the map remains one of the colony's major assets. It is the fastest freight-handling port in the Far East. Most of the cargo is loaded and unloaded by lighters which tie up beside the ships at buoys.

*   *   *

The big banks play their part skilfully and discreetly in Hong Kong's deceptively simple set-up. There have been too many Chinese banks, a proportion of them simply family concerns for real estate financing. Following a bank run in 1965, which the big banks typically resolved with a minimum of governmental intervention and even advice, no bank can be registered without adequate safeguards.

The Hong Kong and Shanghai Banking Corporation acts as an unofficial central bank, issues ninety percent of the colony's notes, and helped out the depositors of the banks that failed in 1965. Hong Kong is part of the sterling area — only, however, since 1941 — yet the Government, while ensuring that the colony does not become an escape route for sterling, withholds the normal exchange controls of the sterling block.

About a score of Hong Kong brokers are able to operate rewardingly by investing transferred capital on Wall Street. Many of these deals are hidden transactions because transfer of capital from, say, Malaysia or Thailand is technically illegal.

All this flexibility and realism helps to explain the steady flow of non-residential deposits into the colony's books, representing an estimated fifty percent of total deposits, which aggregated a record HK$8,405 million in 1966 — or an increase of 15.9 percent over 1965. In Hong Kong the investor enjoys the benefits of a free market in foreign exchange, and is also assured of high returns, freedom from political and racial discrimination, and immunity from official controls and interference. This is the only 'foreign aid' Hong Kong gets.

US investment has been comparatively slow, but there are now more than 700 US companies in the colony, compared with fifty in 1954 — including IBM, Dow Chemicals, Sears Roebuck, hotels and oil, textiles and garments.

The rise in interest rates has also encouraged the rise in deposits. Hong Kong is probably the only place in the world where banking and financial authorities smile on a competitive rise in interest rates.

The Hong Kong dollar has retained its sterling value of around 1s 3d since 1935, despite war, occupation and the influx of refugees.

* * *

That, in brief, is the complex and dynamic apparatus of an outdated but efficient economy and colonial administration which has attracted desperate refugees, shrewd money-makers and a flood of investment capital to continue the expanding Hong Kong miracle.

In 1966, the colony's external trade — imports, exports and re-exports — was worth HK$17,660 million, a fourteen percent increase over 1965. Domestic exports alone were worth HK$5,370 million, another rise of fourteen percent.

Here we plumb the depths of a Sargasso Sea of statistics. If you are uninterested, skim or skip. But the story of Hong Kong cannot be told properly without figures. In 1949, the colony had less than 1,500 registered factories, which employed 81,500 workers. By the end of 1959, there were 5,000 factories with 229,000 workers; by 1966, more than 10,000 factories with a labour force of 600,000. These figures, of course, do not include unregistered 'factories', the hundreds of family concerns, sweating around the clock in slum back-rooms and cellars, the hundreds of job-working units to which the big firms farm out garment-finishing and other rush work. In 1956, there were 300,000 cotton textile spindles in Hong Kong. In 1966, there were nearly 750,000, including some of the most up-to-date equipment in the world.

Textiles now represent more than half the colony's domestic exports, and employ more than forty percent of the industrial labour force. But the variety of other made-in-Hong Kong exports includes plastics, footwear, electric appliances, toys, furniture and lampshades, transistors and aluminium ware, ginger, carved jade and ivory chess sets, canned birds-nest soup, midget vacuum-cleaners and baby refrigerators, paint and lacquerware, wigs and umbrellas, perfume and potable snake-blood, perambulators and chamber-pots, herbal medicine and spitoons, beer and fiery Chinese spirit-wine, quick-frozen shrimps and pork dumplings, incense and firecrackers. Now artificial pearls are being cultivated and silkworm culture is being revived in the New Territories.

It is a record which even Japan's enterprising and versatile post-war *zaibatsu* leaders come to study, marvel at — and invest in.

*   *   *

Today's hard-headed business operators in the Hong Kong Establishment may have become more orthodox than their ancestors were in the opium-running days, but the old drive, individualism, rivalry, enterprise and buccaneering instincts persist. Their interests spread, diversify and multiply. Their influence in governmental affairs and policy remains decisive but discreet, whatever the colour of HM Government in London. Their secrecy over assets and operations is absolute — but purely capitalist, and neither political nor sinister.

The myriad branches of Jardine and Matheson still go back to the deep, dark roots of Dumfriesshire in south Scotland. The Calvinist Jardines concentrated their evangelic commerce in Hong Kong; their Keswick cousins, as we shall see, tried, enjoyed, and then lost their luck in Shanghai. The last time I had the rare privilege of talking with a Jardine-Matheson *taipan* at lunch in the company's Hong Kong penthouse, he said: 'We are just grocers. Just grocers and merchants.' The twentieth century representatives of the old firm are still doing business at the old stand in Hong Kong and new stands in South East Asia — but not, alas, in Shanghai. They may not have the same obvious status as ambassadors and governors which their predecessors rated, but the power, protocol and *noblesse oblige* survive. (Christopher Rand in *Hong Kong: The Island Between* recalls one Jardine man speaking of another: 'When he was agent in Hankow, he was expected, in keeping with Jardine's traditions, to maintain a couple of race ponies, although he hated the sight of a horse.')

Today, Jardine's, its Shanghai holdings surrendered, trades with China, but gets most of its Hong Kong grist from real estate, shipping, transport and other utilities, ferries, insurance, warehouses, gold importing, telephones and aircraft repairing, and owns three of the colony's daily newspapers — the *South China Morning Post,* the afternoon *Mail* and the Sunday *Post-Herald.* (The *Tiger Standard* is owned by Mrs Aw Boon Haw, relict of the famous Tiger Balm king, who lives in an astonishing marble mausoleum near a pagoda in the equally astonishing Tiger Balm marble gardens.)

Another Establishment firm, younger but maybe now larger than Jardine's, is Butterfield and Swire, which operates Cathay Pacific Airways as well as a conglomeration of interests rivalling Jardine's. A nice British colonial gesture was Jardine's invitation to the wife of the Butterfield *taipan* to fire the midnight New Year salute on the ancient Jardine cannon in 1967, which was Butterfield's centenary year. Wheelock Marden, founded by the doughty old Shanghai hand, the late George Marden, is in the gold business with Jardine's, but holds the customary *taipan's* full hand of varied freebooting enterprises.

Other notable pillars of the Hong Kong Establishment are Gilman's, Dodwell's and the Kadoorie brothers. The Kadoories, whose father, Sir Elly (a Baghdad Jew), was in Shanghai with the Sassoons in the eighties, now run Hong Kong's light and power, dockyards and the Peninsula and Repulse Bay hotels, and in a paternalistic role, in the new Hong Kong mood rather than the old Shanghai mood, have helped 300,000 refugees to settle on farms in the New Territories.

But the combination of Hong Kong's freedom and stability and the Establishment's enterprise and solidity would have got nowhere without Chinese industry, versatility, experiment and initiative. All the elements of Chinese commercial genius were present: hard work, technical skill, the gambler's itch, resilience, clan and family ties. If a project doesn't work, discard it; if it does work, put the profits into another project. Good luck, the Chinese hold, must ultimately prevail over bad luck. True, the evil spirits are always abroad, seeking the unwary or the careless, but they can be physically foiled by screens inside gateways, tripped by awkward steps at thresholds, or even run over by fast-moving vehicles if the quarry takes the risk of allowing the vehicle to graze his heel so that his ghostly pursuer will be the victim.

The Chinese work 'on the inside', relying on blood ties and

close friendships rather than on general issue of stock. When entrepot and export trade to China collapsed after the Korean War embargo by the US and UN, the hot money, restless innovation and abundant cheap labour were diverted into a revolution of light industry that broke out on literally a hundred fronts, expanded going concerns and developed likely and unlikely projects which, with equal serenity, were dropped when they failed and promoted when they succeeded.

Artificial flowers, for example, were introduced by one investor who heard that Italy was selling them at from two to four dollars apiece. He had never seen a plastic flower, but he rallied a few friends, secured a sample flower, a mould and some of the new-fangled polyethyline and made a Hong Kong model which would sell for seventy cents. Within a year, the first artificial flower plant had attracted rival factories and the Hong Kong flower industry had commandeered the US market. It has now become one of the main contributors to the colony's booming plastics industry, which in 1966 earned HK$659 million in exports — flowers, toys and dolls, household ware, polypropylene furniture and coated fabrics and sheeting. Ironically, it was a minor strike in the original artificial flower plant which, together with a dispute in a cement factory, was exploited by agitators to touch off the disturbances in May 1967.

Hong Kong operators in light industry, involved separately in different projects, will unite to try a new venture, break up on success or failure, share losses or profits and perhaps link with new partners in another venture. This versatility has its weaknesses and, over a long haul, can affect quality. An industrialist with too many irons in the fire, and too many changing partners in expedient alliances, will tend to watch profits rather than management detail and production finish. This is one of the vulnerable spots in the Hong Kong freebooting miracle. But it is a weakness which is inseparable from the basic conditions of Hong Kong existence — Chinese cohesion, Chinese clannishness, Chinese expedience, Chinese trust.

Personal connections — accepted, although known only at second or even third hand — extend from Hong Kong to contacts in every expatriate ghetto throughout South East Asia, and every large Chinatown from San Francisco to Brazil. A Western visitor can hand a traveller's cheque to a Hong Kong money-changer, who will give him a receipt and an obscure address in Manila, Djakarta, Saigon or Vientiane, where, a week or so later, the traveller will be handed the black market equivalent in pesos, rupiahs, piastres or kip.

These associations extend even across the Hong Kong border into Kwangtung Province and the restless capital of Canton — the one-time headquarters of Sun Yat-sen, of Chiang Kai-shek, of Chou En-lai, sometimes in temporary alliance, sometimes in deadly conflict. Canton's Red Guards have been making their 'cultural' influence felt in the province. But Hong Kong expatriates and family connections maintain their non-ideological contacts with Canton. There are still exiles in Hong Kong who retain shares in Communist enterprises in Canton which require ex-capitalist management and advice, and who get their regular dividends in blocked *yuan*. In theory, this income is subject to taxation by the colonial authorities in Hong Kong.

Recently there was a quiet family reunion in Hong Kong of a venerable top party cadre, who got his travel permit in Canton with neither delay nor questioning, to attend his birthday party with a son who works in a capitalist enterprise in the colony, and another son who flew from Canada, where he holds a high professional post. After the reunion, the father went to Kaitak airport to bid one son and his family bon voyage, said goodbye to the other son and his family in Kowloon, and returned, studying a party report from Hong Kong front men and a family report from his Hong Kong son, to Canton.

A typical Hong Kong success story has been written by the Tang family, which prospered in pre-Communist China with textiles, flour mills and cement. The family head was Hsinghai, educated in America, when the Communists ousted Chiang Kai-shek. He sensed the takeover well in advance, protectively diverted purchases of modern equipment from Shanghai and Hankow to Hong Kong, bought factory lots in the colony a year before 'liberation', and then, only days before the Communists moved into Shanghai, transferred hand-picked workers to the nucleus of the new Tang holdings in Hong Kong. Apparently without pangs or inhibitions, he accepted the inevitable in China and moved his family, life and living, and as many other workers as could accompany him, to Hong Kong. Now the Tangs run South Sea Textiles, one of the most successful and paternalistic industries in the Far East, with air-conditioned factories, free dormitories, a swimming pool, high wages, and educational and medical care for the employees' children.

Tang is not worried about Communist infiltration. He is the Chinese cosmopolite incarnate. His children have been educated at Harvard and Yale. Two of his daughters are married to American professors. But there can be no doubt that, like all expatriate Chinese, his heart remains in China, and that he is happier because he is still living and working, however precariously today, on Chinese soil, rather than in, say, Brazil, where, with his genius, he could have achieved the same material success.

Tang, who often seems to sceptical Westerners to speak in Confucian cliches, once told an American pressman: 'I'm interested in basics — food, shelter and clothing.' His listener did not raise the unworthy query: 'Profits too?' But it could well be that Tang was unconsciously recalling the original basic family interests in the old China of flour, cement and textiles. Intelligent Chinese today, wherever educated, have never cast off their philosophic ties with Confucius.

(An essay could be written on Mao Tse-tung's affinity with Confucius, whom Mao, protesting too much, now affects to deride.)

NO NONSENSE ABOUT DEMOCRACY

To repeat, there is no nonsense about democracy in Hong Kong. Administration and legislation are conducted along unashamedly colonial lines. The only elected representatives are ten members of the Urban Council, counterbalanced by ten nominees of the Governor. The duties and responsibilities of the Urban Council, in any event, were crisply summed up by one Governor as 'supervision of the collection of garbage and of the naming of streets'.

To the distress of local liberals and the incomprehension of visiting socialists from London, there is no articulate political sentiment in the colony and negligible popular interest in a wider franchise or expanded powers for the Urban Council, far less in suicidal demands for 'self-government' — which, if achieved, would lead inevitably to no government at all. Peking's Communists still expediently tolerate the survival of colonial bureaucracy, but the presumptuous presence of a local, elected, independent Chinese government on Chinese soil would be intolerable.

Political apathy in the colony was strikingly illustrated in 1967, after the franchise for the ten elected members of the Urban Council had been daringly increased tenfold, giving 200,000 to 300,000 residents the right to vote (rate-payers, civil servants, members of professional institutes and the like). Only 26,000 bothered to register, and only 10,000 went to the polls — say 39 percent of those registered, but actually less than five percent of those eligible to vote. The response was all the more disappointing for those who want more popular interest and participation in government because the elections followed hot on the heels of the riots, which had helped to deepen and harden popular sympathy for the government and revulsion against trouble-makers and minority demonstrators. And two independent candidates topped the meagre poll, walloping machine. representatives of the Reform Club and the Civic Association, which are paved from head to foot with good intentions and plastered with democratic ideals.

Another weakness is the conspicuous reluctance of intelligent, well-educated Chinese to enter the public service, which has now grown to an army of nearly 71,000 (the total establishment in 1949 was less than 18,000). Wages and pensions for the public service are around HK$620 million a year, or say one-third of total expenditure. But most ambitious young Chinese — reflecting the atmosphere and traditions of Hong Kong — prefer business or, increasingly, a career abroad. Suitable local candidates cannot be found for senior grades in the public service.

The Secretary for Chinese Affairs — a British public servant — directs an organisation which works closely with the elected or natural leaders of some four hundred Chinese associations and societies (not to be confused, of course, with the underworld triads). This is the basic cultural — if that word can be correctly used now outside China — association between the Government and the Chinese. The interests of the Secretariat for Chinese Affairs range from birth control and social services to care of Hong Kong's Chinese temples and family tombs and the anti-narcotics drive. Generally, it does a good job and it is a pity it does not have more staff and more authority.

British constitutional law governs the judiciary, which comprises a Chief Justice, a Senior Puisne Judge and a lower echelon of six puisne judges, eight district judges, twenty-eight magistrates and a President of the Tenancy Tribunal, which deals with disputes between landlords and tenants. Despite changes in English law at home, Hong Kong still hangs and flogs. The colony has had many spectacular murders down the years — a chopper is a useful weapon, always convenient to hand in the humblest home, and operable by man or woman. But the ancient Oriental sport of kidnapping, which flourishes in Malaya, Singapore and Thailand, has never been successful in Hong Kong.

It is recalled that some twelve years ago Premier Chou En-lai, acknowledging Britain's swift and realistic recognition of the new regime, proposed to the then Governor, Sir Alexander Grantham, that Peking should establish diplomatic representation in the colony. It sounded like a reasonable suggestion. But Sir Alexander, a shrewd and deceptively dandyish figure, is said to have remarked: 'I'd resign first. There's no room for two Governors in Hong Kong.' However he phrased his official recommendation to the then Colonial Office, the Chou En-lai proposal was dropped into a dark and dusty pigeon-hole. The idea has never been revived. There are those who believe that its revival is not impossible and could be a portent.

Overall, Hong Kong's Government does a good job. Officially, it is always referred to as 'Government', not as 'the Government'; this, it is insisted implausibly, is not to make it sound like God, but to distinguish it humbly from The Government in Downing Street.

Of course the structure has the in-built faults of all bureaucracies, but the Governor's advisers have always included good brains and trained specialists, and the rare British colonial instinct for selection, encouragement and reward of native big shots has paid off handsomely, culminating in knighthoods for influential Chinese supporters — or perhaps 'partners' is the better word.

Undoubtedly there is corruption in many of the services. There is always 'squeeze', corruption and 'tea money' in any Chinese society — or perhaps, in fairness, one should say *non-Communist* Chinese society. In Communist China, corruption is of the mind, and 'squeeze' is applied to thought and personal liberty rather than to the wallet. It is difficult to know which is the worse form of corruption.

But Hong Kong corruption must be put into proper Oriental perspective: it does not compare with commonplace standards in Manila, Saigon, Bangkok or Djakarta.

THE COMMUNIST STAKE

Hong Kong remains China's chief source of foreign exchange — providing up to fifty percent of the total. On a conservative estimate, China derives up to US$600 million a year from, and through, the colony: $400 million for direct trade and at least $200 million in remittances from overseas Chinese to families and friends inside China.

Communist trading and financial operations are interwoven with Hong Kong governmental and capitalist practice. The remittances, in sterling or dollars, are received by the Bank of China or one of the other fourteen Communist-controlled banks in the colony, which hold the exchange and send credit vouchers for the purchase of goods and services to the recipients.

There is also regular Communist income from property investment and rentals, departmental stores, movie houses, bars and other enterprises. The value of British property holdings is known to have shrunk substantially in recent years, and certainly some of the transfers have been made to Communist interests. Communist investment outside the banks and official agencies is usually hidden by a non-Communist front, although the identity of one key puppet director can reveal the real top command.

The Bank of China, of which more later, is in charge of Communist financial affairs and exchange control in Hong Kong. Number 1 trading agency is the China Resources Corporation, which deals through various foreign firms in the colony, and often through the same Chinese merchants who traded with Chiang Kai-shek's Nationalists. Imports from foreign countries are largely wheat from Australia and Canada, and modern machinery, factory plants, steel tubing, fertiliser and so on. The principal goods which China exports abroad through Hong Kong are silk, textiles, rice, oil and oilseeds, bristles, foodstuffs and cheap consumer goods.

Hong Kong is China's only rewarding bridgehead with the

rest of the world and China's most convenient springboard for export dumping forays into South East Asia. Already China has given warning of a socialist state's ability to flood a market with cheap products of good quality like bicycles, sewing machines, clothing, radios and canned goods, which have sold at half the price even of Japanese-made products in South East Asian countries.

These campaigns have not been sustained because of China's own industrial shortcomings and political upheaval at home, the needs of her huge population, the diversion of capital to a crash nuclear programme, and the lack of properly trained technicians and managers. But the resources and the potential are there in abundance, and the emergence of China as a giant trading nation is only a matter of time, ideological commonsense and managerial reform. The Chinese people are too adaptable, too industrious and too enterprising to be denied indefinitely a cruelly delayed higher standard of living.

Hong Kong's success is the living evidence of what Chinese labour and talent, given free opportunity, can achieve even in artificial conditions, under foreign administrators, and with a nineteenth-century economic system.

If Hong Kong is the chief centre for the world's China watchers, prohibited from entering the mainland, so, conversely, the colony is China's most useful point of contact with the foreign devils outside the Middle Kingdom. Behind the official party front men there is a faceless miscellany of party cadres and activists who can use Hong Kong as a listening-post.

Party commissars, elderly and happy, live in bourgeois comfort, awakened in the dark hours only by sweating nightmares that they may be recalled to the homeland. The party has invested in property, tourist hotels and even Suzie Wong bars on the Wanchai waterfront. There are Communist supermarkets — one of which has recently been displaying expensive objects of art which are presumably some of the private property looted or 'liberated' on the mainland by the Red Guard thugs.

These supermarkets sell a wide variety of consumer goods (usually, but not always, low-priced), which range from textiles to canned foods and goldfish, and from sewing machines to pottery and fake antiques. Business is conducted on a starkly capitalist basis; the manager orders what he needs, sets the prices for the store and is paid a commission. One such managerial cadre was so good at capitalist-style salesmanship that he turned his back on Chairman Mao and accepted a top post with an old-established British firm in the colony.

Hong Kong has been buying water regularly from China, although in a severe emergency it could survive on strict rationing without this supply. Despite the disturbances, this supply has been smoothly resumed. (Originally the Canton authorities offered to supply the water free of charge, but the Hong Kong government civilly sidestepped this propaganda gesture.)

Convoys of junks from Canton, flying the Communist yellow star flag, tie up in the harbour with cargoes of pigs, poultry, vegetables and fruit. Above their patched and painted sails, a British Big John Company cannon fires a colonial signal precisely at noon each day.

There are Communist-led unions affiliated with the Federation of Trade Unions (which has direct links with its masters in Canton), and there are Nationalist unions affiliated with the Trades Union Council (which has direct links with its masters in Formosa.) Bookstalls display copies of the Peking *People's Daily* and the red bible of Chairman Mao's 'Quotations', side by side with copies of the Nationalist *Sing Tao*, the *Reader's Digest, China Reconstructs* and *Playboy*.

On the Communists' 'liberation' day, October 1, Hong Kong's homes, shops and buildings burst dutifully into displays of Communist flags and decorations and giant coloured pictures of Chairman Mao — seemingly rejuvenated by Peking monkey-glands. Nine days later, on the Nationalists' day, the Double Ten, the homes, shops and buildings burst dutifully into displays of Nationalist flags and decorations and giant coloured pictures of Generalissimo Chiang Kai-shek — similarly rejuvenated by Taipeh monkey-glands. Some of this political celebration is of course loyal and sincere; but undoubtedly much of it is expedient and calculated — reflecting the wise ambivalence of the old Aberdeen woman who always bobbed her head in kirk when Satan's name was mentioned: 'Because, after all, ye canna be sure, can ye?'

There is a pleasing Hong Kong legend that Chinese printers produce a handy reversible double-faced rotogravure job with Chairman Mao on one side and Generalissimo Chiang on the other. (The only photographs of Mao and Chiang which I have inspected had on the back the inscription 'Made in Japan'.)

Chinese Communist agents and Chinese Nationalist agents operate in Hong Kong. They do not, however, confront one another in crowded streets or joss-houses with bombs and daggers. Hong Kong's efficient Special Branch — assisted by quiet tip-offs by each side against the other — regularly unearths small arsenals of firearms, ammunition, grenades, explosives, arson equipment and primitive James Bond geegaws in slum dumps and cocklofts. Regularly, also, small groups of men, who have been detained without formal charge or trial or any concern for *habeas corpus*, are quietly deported to Formosa. This unconstitutional behaviour, like the absence of free voting and lack of lip service to democracy, drives visiting British Socialist Members of Parliament crazy, and they are continually getting up and blowing off in the Commons about the imminence of revolution unless democracy is established in the fairest jewel in Britain's colonial crown.

Occasionally — not so often — there have been similar deportations of Communist agents, but their operations *so far* have not involved the arsenals which the Nationalists wish to smuggle into China for sabotage. The most embarrassing case was the discovery that a trusted Chinese superintendent in the Hong Kong police administration was a highly trained spy.

He must have been a talented fellow because he ended up as an instructor in a Canton university, although he was not, so far as is known, teaching espionage.

In happier days, there was even a measure of unofficial cooperation between the police of Hong Kong, Macao and China. On one celebrated occasion, a murderer with no political convictions fled from Hong Kong to Macao and then, when extradition processes were in train, made his way across the border to Canton. The British issued 'Man Wanted' notices with picture, which the Macao newspapers carried. A week later, the Chinese Communists thrust the wretched killer back into Macao, where he cut his throat in a hotel bedroom as the police moved in.

The eccentric British — or rather the *English* — can sometimes confuse both the Chinese Communists and the Nationalists, to say nothing of the Americans, in Hong Kong. The birth pangs of the new Hongkong Hilton, an altogether admirable hostelry, provide instructive insight into inter-racial subtleties in the colony. British Old Hands instinctively supported irrational criticism by local Chinese of the innocent title 'Opium Den' for one of the hotel's cabarets. It was changed to 'The Den'. Local Chinese opinion instinctively supported irrational criticism by the Old Hands of the innocent display of the Texan flag above the hotel. It was hauled down and replaced by the Union Jack. Then Old Hands and local Chinese Communists and Nationalists alike united in rational and innocent amusement over a stern warning by the United States consulate that the Hilton management was violating US law by displaying expensive murals, scrolls and screens which lacked essential 'Certificates of Origin', and could therefore have been dangerous products of subversive Communist Chinese craftsmen. They were sullenly removed and, at latest reports, were still mouldering away in waterfront godowns.

Approximately one hundred pressmen and employees of the fearless New China News Agency (Peking's Tass) live in gloomy seclusion — lightened only by mass chanting of Mao's thoughts and stimulating bouts of self-criticism — at the Agency's Orwellian dormitory building, where unknown visitors are vetted through a Chinese Judas window. The press boys seldom surface at the Press Club or at press conferences, and indeed none have been sighted between the 1966 'cultural' climax and 1967, when they were shaken by wild surmise about the rapidly changing identities of their bosses at home office, to whom they transmit their faithfully documented distortions and misrepresentation of the Hong Kong scene.

The Bank of China towers beside the Hong Kong and Shanghai Bank, matching its imperial, Shanghai-style lions with Chinese socialist lions, and casting an ominous shadow in the afternoon over the western end of the Hong Kong Cricket Club's pitch. The Bank is Peking's party and diplomatic headquarters, as well as its financial heart, in Hong Kong. Nearly all the banks in the colony maintain armed guards; some of them give the strong impression that in a crisis they would be more likely to shoot themselves than hold-up gangs; but the uniformed Bank of China guards, with their carbines on their shoulders, have a disciplined military bearing and carefully scrutinise all foreign visitors. The Bank's premises have of course no diplomatic privileges, but the manner of a blandly arrogant staff implies that this immunity is taken for granted.

The Bank maintains a large staff, but several floors which could be earning useful rentals are unoccupied. There are anonymous offices in which fraternal states conduct mysterious business; there is, for example, the Hong Kong unregistered headquarters of the Democratic Republic of North Vietnam, which has no sign on the frosted-glass door behind which, it is said, Hanoi's 'trading and cultural operations' are administered.

The Bank itself, as already indicated, is strategically located in a corner of Hong Kong's Statue Square, huddled next to the Hong Kong Shanghai Bank, the Supreme Court and the Hilton

Hotel, and — as was made manifest during the 1967 riots — is literally only a stone's throw, or an acid-bottle's throw, from St John's Cathedral, the Hong Kong Club and the Cricket Club.

Rumours recur that the Bank is an arsenal of small arms, grenades and ammunition, with reserve stocks of rice and other food sufficient to withstand a siege for three months — although in what circumstances it is difficult to imagine. Naive newcomers to the colony are gravely shown two top-floor windows alight all night, where it is whispered Peking's picked agents brood and plot, but where probably watchmen are gloomily munching a supper of noodles and fish, or happily reciting Chairman Mao's 'thoughts'.

The Bank was 'on active service' for the first time during the May riots of 1967. Able-bodied bank staff were massed on the sidewalks and occasionally, under bawled instructions from loud-speakers on the Bank's parapets, chased and roughed-up passers-by. The insults to the police and incitements to violence emitted by these loud-speakers were finally jammed by louder governmental mobile equipment which broadcast stirring Chinese opera — a delicate riposte in a confrontation unprecedented in Hong Kong's history.

It is useful to remember that, although the Bank is now Communist, it was originally designed by the Chinese Nationalists as a symbolic warning of the overriding suzerainty of China over Hong Kong, whose colonial status affronted the Nationalist Chinese pride just as much as it now nettles Communist Chinese pride.

Mr T. V. Soong, Chiang Kai-shek's brother-in-law and adviser, approved the height of the building, which is twenty feet higher than the roof of the Hong Kong and Shanghai Bank. Then the Nationalists passed from the scene, and the Communists proceeded to complete the building and to persuade most of the Nationalist-appointed staff to remain.

The Communists had some trouble with the two Chinese lions which they set up at revolutionary attention outside their

front door to shame the reclining imperialist lions outside
the former Hong Kong and Shanghai Bank, a block away.
It was generally agreed that the party-line lions were relatively
unimpressive. So substitutes of larger dimensions and more
ferocious appearance, modelled on lions outside the Forbidden
City, were hacked from white stone by Hong Kong artisans and
now dominate the party bank's marble entrance.

The significance of this rivalry is that the chauvinistic front
was Chinese and not ideological. The Nationalists would have
done the same, just as Chiang Kai-shek would today have been
taking the same line as Mao Tse-tung over Tibet, Mongolia,
the Indian frontier and Formosa.

China's stake in Hong Kong is, quite naturally, national
pride as well as commercial advantage. The first influence will
be more durable and, in the long run, stronger than the second.
But how long is the long run?

RIOTS AND XENOPHOBIA

A mob is an ugly mob anywhere in the world. Any mob anywhere in Asia — whatever its original motivation or excuse,
and whether it is spontaneous or regimented—becomes xenophobic and instinctively adds Westerners to its targets. Any
foreigner who gets accidentally caught up in rioting in an Asian
city — Tokyo, Djakarta, Manila, Hong Kong, Singapore or
Saigon — learns this lesson the hard way.

There were doleful protests by foreigners, including naive
longtime residents, when the Kowloon mobs, having taken over
the streets with stones and knives, fire and iron, in 1956, gave
special attention to the trusting white stranger in their midst.
There was no Communist incitement in that violence, which
caused many deaths and widespread destruction, martial law and
suspension of traffic between Hong Kong and Kowloon, and
led to thousands of arrests. The aggrieved cry went up: 'They
don't like us!' To the natural query, 'Why should they?'

there was a shocked silence.

The riots I have witnessed in Asian cities other than Hong Kong were Communist-fomented; passing or trapped foreigners were obviously not card-carrying party members or even sympathisers. Hong Kong's riots in the past had been simply uprisings of discontent or extensions of labour brawls between strikers and police, and were swiftly taken over by thugs, hoodlums, looters, frustrated adolescents and leaders of the colony's triads or criminal secret societies. The mob picked out the foreigner as an alien and natural enemy, no matter how generous a provider he might have been for his faithful cookboy or *amah*, no matter how regularly and selflessly he might have contributed to the colony's lotteries and the Jockey Club's sweepstakes for the promotion of social welfare. Indeed, the more active he was on these fronts the more subversive an enemy he was, because he was emasculating honest Chinese and making Oriental Uncle Toms out of them.

But something new was added in May 1967, when for the first time the Communists were not only identified with the demonstrations and riots in Hong Kong, but actually planned and organised them. They exploited a couple of minor strikes, intimidated students in leftist schools and apprentices in leftist factories, paid children to throw stones and paid killers to make, plant and throw bombs, quietly brought in over a three-month period young trained activists from Macao and Canton, and — decisive move — invoked the 'cultural revolution' and the sanctified dogma of Chairman Mao for the overthrow of 'British fascism, imperialism and tyranny' in Hong Kong.

Hong Kong will never be quite the same again after that shock.

No one knows how deeply the Peking regime, tortured with its own power-struggle and pandemonium at home, was involved at the outset. Involved or not, the top party brass must have been dismayed by the miscalculation which their representatives, brandishing the infallible red books of Chairman Mao's thoughts, had clearly committed. It is a reasonable assumption that the error was not made — nor the venture wholeheartedly supported — by the old brigade of sagacious resident party front men. Canton, after much unrest and internecine brawling, had at last established a pro-Maoist provincial government, and, exporting the 'cultural revolution' for the first time, had forced the Portuguese authorities in Macao into humiliating capitulation. The temptation to attempt an encore in Hong Kong must have been irresistible.

The tactical failure does not affect the strategic prospects. At this time there was no popular support for the ideological offensive. Firm government action, a strong calm governor, masterly police restraint, UK backing, and angry, decisive *Chinese* revulsion against the party's excesses subdued and halted the assault. The danger is that the serious reverse for Mao's 'unending-revolutionary' doctrine may have cost too much loss of face, and that pragmatic concern for China's stake in Hong Kong will be outweighed by a blind ideological and plain go-to-hell reaction in the Politburo — or among those Politburo members who can still sit down together with an affectation of fraternal trust.

By the time these fragmentary notes are between covers, Peking may have decided to discard its expedient tolerance of the colony and, instead of a prudent, long-range policy of niggling strikes and steady recruitment of Hong Kong's teenagers, may have authorised more precipitate action (considered later in 'Hong Kong Tomorrow'). The best one can say is that the first and prudent course of action is certain, and that the second and impatient course at the moment looks unlikely.

Nothing is more certain than that there will be more labour disputes in Hong Kong. The colony is a turbulent and explosive Asian industrial centre, whose people want more reward for their work and mean to get it. If the Communists retreat to more cautious tactics, they are also likely to consider them better. The British, one hopes, will progress to a swifter and more equitable sharing of the colony's income.

Bluntly, the May 1967 plot did not fail because the Chinese younger generation, who will determine Hong Kong's future (granted ideological freedom over the next decade or so), loved the British more, but because they loved the Communists less.

Hong Kong is China. The foreigner is always an intruder, often tolerated, sometimes liked, often distrusted, seldom accepted. It has been well argued that while an Oriental intellectual can master Occidental languages, reasoning and philosophy, and retain his Oriental essence, the Occidental who becomes an 'authority' on Oriental esoterica and the Oriental 'mind' leaves off being an Occidental without becoming an Oriental. It's hard luck for the Westerner. . . .

I recall one glittering US reception in Japan during the heady days of General MacArthur's occupation. The lawns were thronged with respectful masses of what the Supreme Commander was wont to describe in official declarations as 'the indigenous personnel'.

'I knew we would win the peace as well as the war', a high-ranking US commander remarked to me. 'The Japs have learned to appreciate our way of life. They recognise democracy. They're not fools — I've always said that. They learn. We'll build an American-style freedom and civilisation here.' His honest face was beaming with unselfish delight as he gulped bourbon.

Behind us, two charming middle-aged Japanese ladies in *kimono* halted to accept with deep bows some more US army-issue orange juice. They were chatting casually in Japanese as rashly as any Westerner who assumes that no Asian within earshot can understand a word of English.

'I do believe,' one observed, 'that the type of Occupation officer we are getting now has a less brutal and criminal type of face than those who came here in 1945.' Her companion, inclining her head gracefully in our direction, suggested: 'Or perhaps it is that we are becoming more accustomed to the faces?'

They passed on, bowing modestly to us, and my friend innocently saluted them. 'Always show them respect,' he adjured me. 'It makes them respect us. . .'

They told a story in Peking in 1957, before the great split and the departure of the Soviet experts, about the Chinese detective who proudly reported to a comrade the arrival of a Soviet adviser on secret-police work:

'He is as tall as a pagoda, with a chest like a water-buffalo, feet like temple stones, and a fist like the Great Wall.'

'But how is he here?' inquired the comrade, tapping his forehead.

'Well, he is after all,' the detective conceded reasonably, 'a Russian.'

THE WALL AND THE HOUSES

In 1949, while recovering after Japan's invasion and occupation, the colony was suddenly confronted with the Communist 'liberation' of China, bringing another flood of 'White Chinese' exiles and refugees (*pai hua,* as the Chinese call them); and two years later came the US embargo on entrepot trade from China.

The Japanese destroyed Western colonialism in South East Asia but failed to destroy British colonialism in Hong Kong. Mao's revolution imposed Communism on China, but — for whatever reason or combination of reasons — has not yet chosen to impose Communism on Hong Kong.

No one could have forecast that reprieve in the early fifties. The colony seemed doomed as the population was swollen by an additional hundred thousand every month, with no homes, no jobs, no real prospects. Then came the big operators from Shanghai, those Chinese who had made brutal capitalism pay in one lost colonial enclave, and who preferred to re-invest what they had been able to salvage in another capitalist enclave rather than accept the blessings and opportunities of Maoist Marxism-Leninism.

They were, the Communists said, rats leaving a sinking ship, and they were swimming hard to another ship which, if not already foundering, had sprung a thousand leaks and was rotten-ready for the breakers. But Shanghai money and enterprise, plus the industry and talent of the humbler refugees, kept the second ship afloat and put it back into freebooting business, still improbably flying the Union Jack and still faithful to RN discipline, protocol and traditions.

The Year of the Sheep, 1953, marked the first revolutionary 'post-liberation' decree by Hong Kong, and the first retreat by the colonial authorities on the *laisser-faire* politico-economic front. The decree said that immigration must be restricted, that the continuing flow of refugees must be stemmed, that China must accept a colonial barrier, a sort of Oriental Berlin Wall, *against* the influx of ungrateful expatriates. The Hong Kong Wall was not set up only to defend a colonial residue and its vested capitalist interests, but also and primarily to prevent poverty, unemployment and starvation from spreading through an area which, after all, was still technically a British possession, however vulnerable.

The second readjustment was equally revolutionary. A Resettlement Department was established: the Colonial Government admitted its responsibility for the housing and sheltering of the refugees and, by so doing, also admitted its correlated responsibility for education, medical care, social welfare and improved living standards. It was the first retreat from *laisser-faire*. It was not to be the last.

With all its defects and trial-by-error, the Hong Kong resettlement programme has been one of the world's most notable efforts in modern communal housing. In twelve years nearly 900,000 people have been resettled at a total cost to the Government alone of HK$670 million. Designs for the huge housing blocks have been improved and modernised. Of the nineteen resettlement estates, the biggest houses 88,000 people; a larger project, now approaching completion, will house 170,000.

Basic allocation is 24 square feet per adult.   Rents in the newer blocks average HK$35 a month, or say 8.75 percent of the income of an average family, whose two working members would earn perhaps $400 a month.

Naturally, Government operations have affected private investment in housing.   The Government's low rental projects undercut private enterprise; even so, private builders have provided homes for one million people in the decade ending 1965.

By normal Western standards, the Hong Kong housing blocks, even the latest, could not be termed luxurious or spacious, but they are better than Shanghai's or Peking's Communist efforts at re-housing.   And plenty of dwellers in Glasgow's Gorbals, London's East End and New York's Harlem would prefer them.   As in Shanghai, the contrast should not be with today's standards in non-slum Western cities, but must be with yesterday's standards in Hong Kong — and Shanghai.

A paradox, peculiarly Chinese, is that some of the squatters prefer their self-built makeshift huts, with horrible sanitation, hand-drawn water and fire hazards, to the communal re-housing units.   Hong Kong people, as a rule, keep rent to a rock-bottom minimum and the squatter huts do offer more privacy and a greater sense, however pathetic, of family and individual proprietorship than the standardised units do.

Private interests are reluctant to invest in low-cost housing schemes.   Tenants whose wages have risen are slow to move to better premises: they prefer a telephone, household gadgets, improved education for their children, or — a far more impressive symbol than a new address — a motor car

There are sporadic attempts to press the Government to subsidise low-cost housing by private interests, but nothing worthwhile would have been attempted had the Government not launched and sustained its own resettlement programmes. Private investors in housing all want the usual three to five-year return on capital from luxury apartments and ultra-modern skyscraper blocks, which are mushrooming in choice residential areas.

All Government resettlement estates have privately operated schools, which pay nominal rental, and some of which are subsidised by the Government. In the original re-housing blocks, these schools are on the roofs or ground floors, in the new blocks they are in annexes.

However, apart from the legal and illegal entrants, who still average around 20,000, the natural increase is 100,000 a year, and 150,000 children between the ages of six and twelve do not get even primary education. (This is tentatively promised in subsidised schools in four years' time.)

Approximately half the population is under fifteen years of age. Many children are out of school at fourteen, but official legislation keeps them out of registered employment until they are sixteen.

Behind the Wall, Hong Kong has left off being a city of adults. And however good the houses, no one — least of all the parents — is quite sure what sort of adults the children will grow up to be.

SWEATED LABOUR?

By Western standards, the Hong Kong worker, the colony's greatest asset, is overworked and underpaid. But by Asian standards he is not badly off, and his wage scale and living conditions are improving. Life here for most workers is hard, as it is in most Asian cities.

Of approximately 1,500,000 workers in Hong Kong, more than 600,000 are engaged in manufacturing industries. Two basic points: first, there is no unemployment in Hong Kong; second, average daily wages in 1967 were double the 1958 level. There is currently a labour shortage in Hong Kong, but because of the high proportion of youth and the number of children leaving school, there is likely to be a labour surplus in a few years. India and Singapore have similar prospects.

Most men employed in industry work up to ten hours a day six days a week. Women work a 48-hour week. There are customarily six annual holidays a year, and regulations provide for limited overtime and rest periods for women and young persons. Daily wages for the manufacturing industry are 8.50 to 28 dollars for skilled workers, 5.50 to 21 dollars for semi-skilled, and 4.80 to 12 dollars for unskilled. (Sixteen HK dollars to the pound sterling.)

Many employers provide their workers with free accommodation, meal allowances, good-attendance bonuses and paid rest days, as well as a Chinese New Year bonus of one month's pay. To repeat, these wages must of course be considered in terms of Asian living standards. On that basis, the average Hong Kong worker is far better off than any other Asian workers except those in Japan and possibly Singapore. Wages for skilled and unskilled workers in Formosa are only half the minimum Hong Kong rates.

Wage costs in Hong Kong industry are also helped by the operation of round-the-clock shifts, although night work cuts back the proportion of women workers, who must keep daytime hours.

If there was a genuine trade union movement in Hong Kong, conditions and wages would naturally be better. The Government trains some union leaders in the methods, ideals and practices of Western unionism, but there is as little local interest in these obscure alien tricks as there is in Western democratic processes. Of the colony's registered trade unions, 63 are affiliated with the Federation of Trade Unions, which is Communist-led, and 62 with the Trade Union Council, which has strong Nationalist sympathies. Of another fifty-odd unattached unions, half give moral backing to the Federation and the other half to the Council. Generally, the leftist unions are entrenched in shipyards, public utilities, textiles and fishing; the rightists in the building and catering trades. Some industries maintain rival leftist and rightist unions and workers who will have a part of neither side and keep out of any union. All told, there are about 167,000 registered unionists. Workers in small crafts, cottage industries, family concerns and so on tend to remain outside unions.

Another basic point: More than 10,000 small factories, each with less than 200 workers, employ more than half Hong Kong's industrial labour force.

There is a Hong Kong Government Labour Department which, by general consent, has inadequate powers and, in conformity with the *laisser-faire* traditions of the colony, seldom displays initiative, imagination or flexibility in handling labour disputes, which — with newly developed Communist mischief-making — can be expected to become more explosive and dangerous.

The aristocrats of the Hong Kong labour market are the tough and skilful scaffolding workers, who can earn as much as HK$120 a day (about £7.10.0 or US$21). But their profitable and dangerous work comes in bursts. They have their own specialised training courses, and fathers hand on their knowledge to their sons.

A typical salaried white-collar worker, who must rely on his own efforts in making a professional career, studies as hard in his spare time as only, it seems, an ambitious Chinese — or Japanese — can and will. Having had secondary education, he will take perhaps two courses at night school after his work has finished — English, say, and a special subject. If he is good enough and lucky enough, and also takes on additional part-time work, he may be earning, after this teenage cramming, up to HK$1,000-1,200 a month before he is thirty. Of this, rent could take $300 or 400. If he wished to save and continue his studies he could not afford to marry until he was in his thirties. He would probably be contributing also to the support of a father or mother.

There is no real middle class in Hong Kong. In the average

modern office, specialised work is concentrated in a small, relatively well paid managerial group at the top, and the routine work is performed by a large mass of relatively low paid clerks at the bottom. When there is room at the bottom — or in the middle — the vicious stipulation is apt to appear in the 'situations vacant' classified advertisement column: 'State salary expected'.

In the depths, there is a horrible combination of slum living, grinding labour and charity. Here is a specimen budget for a widow with three children, whose monthly income is 50 Hong Kong dollars (under £4): 30 dollars for ironing clothes at from 50 cents to 2 dollars a day, plus 20 dollars from some charity like St James' Settlement. Rent will take perhaps 10 dollars, for bed space in a cubicle; food (rice, vegetables and fish) perhaps 15 dollars, augmented by food handouts from the Social Welfare Department; capital expenses (i.e. charcoal for heating the laundry iron), say 8 dollars; children's education, 12 dollars, plus 5 dollars for school uniforms. There goes the 50 dollars. Clothing generally comes free and second-hand from the St James' Settlement, scrap wood can be gathered for fuel for cooking, and there is free medical treatment at a Government clinic.

*　　*　　*

On the technical side, the colony's freebooting, free-trading, free-working traditions are mainly responsible for the distressing absence of those detailed official statistics and graphs on national income, cost and wage percentages, gross national product and growth, and all the rest of the twentieth-century economist's jargon which are now on tap in Western countries, correct to a decimal point at the touch of a computer button. Hong Kong has been too busy working to give proper attention to recording and codifying. This statistical deficiency is now overdue for correction. It is clear that overseas investors, who lack the built-in confidence of overseas Chinese, want reliable data on what makes Hong Kong run, and how in fact — and figure — it does so.

Thanks to the enterprising Hong Kong weekly, the *Far Eastern Economic Review*, it is possible at least to give some preliminary estimates of Hong Kong's vital statistics, which, even if they are based on calculations for 1961-2, provide instructive background to Hong Kong's labour wages and costs. According to these calculations (made by a Senior Lecturer in Hong Kong University, Mr E. R. Chang), the value of the colony's textile production was then HK$401.8 million, of which wages accounted for 74.7 percent and depreciation 13.1, leaving 12.2 percent profit. Wearing apparel and made-up textiles (mixed up confusingly with footwear) were worth $164.4 million, of which wages took 82.5 percent and depreciation a niggling 2.7 percent, leaving a profit of 14.8 percent. Construction, which was worth $394.3 million (or 6.2 percent of the Gross Domestic Product), paid 63.1 percent in wages and 3.7 percent in depreciation, leaving 33.2 percent for profit.

Apart from evidence of the relative proportion of wages to income and profit, these calculations reveal how inadequate generally is the amount set aside for depreciation, except in textile manufacturing. For those who wish to get their teeth into other solid figures, the Hong Kong estimates of Gross National Product per head is compared below with similar — but official — figures for other countries in Asia and the Far East in 1964:

Gross National Product per head in 1964.

Australia	US$1,503
Japan	532
Hongkong (1960-61)	351
(1961-62)	373
Malaya	287
Philippines	184

Formosa	153
Ceylon	138
South Korea	126
Thailand	103
Pakistan	82
India	75
Burma	58

THE FOUR BESTS

Eat at Kwangchow [Canton]: the best food. Dress at Hangchow: the best silk. Marry at Soochow: the best girls. Die at Liuchow: the best wood for coffins.

So runs the old Chinese code for life and death. It is a definition of Hong Kong, which provides the four essentials in combination. Hong Kong food is the best Chinese food in Asia (with the exception of Taipeh). Hong Kong shops are the most glamorous and the cheapest. Hong Kong girls are the prettiest. Hong Kong coffins, which the traditionally minded keep under their beds for eventual transportation to a resting place in China, are made of Liuchow wood.

Forget politics and economics and the Red Guards and colonialism and even refugees' shacks. Hong Kong is 'Instant China'.

The best time to visit the colony is between mid-October and January, when the sun is mild, the sky is blue, and the nights are crisp. By May the rainy season should be ushering in the torrid summer. Typhoons may be expected from June through September, and, although like severe earthquakes in Japan they make interesting conversation pieces on return home, they are more entertaining in retrospect than in experience.

For colour and excitement, but also discomfort and inconvenience, the Chinese New Year, which is a movable feast and may occur any time between late January and late February, is the Chinese highlight of the year. It is probably a good time for the tourist to stay away — unless he is the adventurous type like those who derived excitement from the 1967 riots. The lacquered veneer of modern British administration cracks open, and the old traditional China takes command of the colony with a bedlam of firecrackers and crowded restaurants, closed shops and a taxi famine, and a non-stop saturnalia of explosions, processions, gongs, whistles, bands, the incessant crash and clatter of mahjong tiles, and the clanging bells of over-worked fire engines... not for ten minutes at midnight, but day and night-long for four days and four nights. Noise: the Chinese love it.

The Western barbarians cower in their servantless, foodless houses, pay an extra month's wages to everyone, and distribute cash gifts in red envelopes; some write naive letters to the *South China Morning Post,* pointing out that firecrackers blind children, terrify dogs and pets and set fire to houses; the few wise expatriates throw aside their inhibitions and try to join in the deafening revelry.

All Chinese must pay their debts before New Year's Eve. Prices soar. Barbers charge double. Street stalls bourgeon with cherry blossom, chrysanthemums, dahlias, camellias and six-foot high peach trees. Every door — even those of the squatters' huts — is emblazoned with red paper scrolls wishing long life and happiness. Every house is filled with flowers. Families and friends exchange visits in new clothes, carrying gifts of ginger, fruit, goldfish, candle-lit paper lanterns, lotus and water-melon seeds, and sticky New Year cakes and dumplings. '*Kung Hai Fat Choy!*' ('Happy New Year and may you make a fortune!') is the four-day war-cry of four million people.

Hong Kong's modern showrooms and arcades and endless rows of small shops in the narrow colonnaded streets sell everything from jade and silks to tinned seaweed at prices which are among the lowest in the world. Prices are rising, but in general cameras, typewriters, watches, binoculars, fountain pens, cultured pearls, transistor radios, all kinds of cloth and clothing, linen, toys, embroidery, leather goods and furniture are available in quantity and quality at bargain rates — frequently cheaper than in the countries of manufacture and origin. The visitor does not bargain in the big stores, where the prices are fixed and can be compared with those in rival stores. But at street stalls and in the steep, winding, back alleys like Cat Street (correctly Upper and Lower Lascar Rows), where occasional sniffs of opium mingle with the less agreeable Asian aromas, haggling is essential and expected. Conversely, it is wiser to pay more than less for a tailored suit.

The *cheongsam,* that lovely, thigh-slit gown which originally came from Shanghai, and which only the Chinese feminine figure can sustain and adorn, gleams, glitters and reveals at its best in Hong Kong. In 1965 there was a furtive renaissance of a sort in Shanghai — the maverick among the 'liberated' cities of China — but the Red Guards soon got their shears to work and have again reduced the Shanghai women to the same drab, sexless appearance as that of other emancipated Chinese women. One of the first casualties in any Communist takeover anywhere is feminine beauty.

It is not only the Chinese Communists who disapprove of the elegant *cheongsam.* Some Western pedants — usually myopic and surly — insist that *cheongsam* is Cantonese for any long, outer robe worn by men or women, and that the fashionable woman's gown now called the *cheongsam* is really a shameful bastardisation of the *kei po,* or Manchu riding habit, which, slit to the hips, was worn — prudishly over long trousers — by noble ladies of the Court on horseback. In other words, it was a sister to the *ao-dai,* or Vietnamese style of flowing coloured robe over silken pantaloons. (Out of favour, needless to say, in Communist North Vietnam.)

These of course are esoteric and captious objections. A *cheongsam* is a *cheongsam* is a *cheongsam.* And wherever they came from, Hong Kong is now their spiritual home, and they are one of the supreme adornments to Hong Kong life and living.

With the possible exception of Taipeh, where the now elderly master chefs of wealthy Chinese who fled from the Communists have set up kitchens, the best Chinese food in the world is in varied and calorific abundance in Hong Kong. It would be possible for a restless gourmet, eating out in Hong Kong, to dine superbly and at moderate cost for a month at a different restaurant each night — northern or Peking style, Szechuanese (hot and peppery), Shanghai style, Cantonese or Hankow style.

The visitor should enjoy, but not restrict himself to, the more orthodox sharks-fin soup, chicken and walnut, sweet and sour pork, spring rolls, beancurd and Peking duck; he should also sample luscious Beggar's Chicken (chicken stuffed with chestnuts, herbs and shredded cabbage, wrapped in lotus leaves and baked for eight hours in a special clay which lines Chinese wine casks), spiced Szechuan duck and steam bread (instead of rice), bear's paw, steamed stork and 'dragon crystals' (a descriptive name for the internal organs of rare fish shipped from Siberian waters). In autumn, there is stewed snake — which, as all good snake-eaters know, should be ordered in combinations of three or five different varieties and washed down with a tot or two of snake's blood.

In short, the four human weaknesses of eating and living, loving and dying, can be enjoyed to the full in Hong Kong — with gusto or discretion.

IN STRANGE TASTE

It is widely believed in the West that ancient Chinese millionaires, driven by insatiable Oriental lust, spend most of the day devouring powdered rhinoceros horn and well-ground tiger bones, washed down by flagons of a fiery Korean herbal beverage, *ginseng.*

I must report personally that all the venerable Chinese millionaires whom I have had the honour of knowing seem to eat only sparingly and even grudgingly of orthodox food, and in general to lead an austere and harassed life. I have never once seen a rhinoceros horn on a Hong Kong banquet table, or even hidden discreetly among the three-hundred-year preserved eggs and monkey's brains on a side-table.

However, according to the colony's gourmet grapevine, there is a flourishing if unadvertised Hong Kong traffic in rhinoceros horns, which in a good vintage year can command up to HK$16,000 apiece. Apparently you scrape, hack or trim the pick-me-up with a small razor-sharp dagger. The tenderer the rhinoceros horn, the stronger and firmer the result — so they say. A rhinoceros horn connoisseur can easily detect the difference between the delicate bouquet of a Kenya horn and the earthier Tanzanian variety. The South African product is rejected as insipid and pretentious.

There was an unfortunate scandal in Hong Kong, a year or so ago, when newspaper accusations were made that lewd merchants in New Zealand — of all places — were exporting tons of deer antlers to Hong Kong for preparation as a powdered tonic with 'restorative properties' rivalling the attraction of rhinoceros horn powder for elderly infirm Chinese. One popular English-language newspaper ran the poster: 'NZ Floods Hong Kong With Sex Stimulants'.

The New Zealand trade authorities in Hong Kong strongly denied this impeachment. It was admitted that New Zealand did ship about two tons of deer antlers each year to Hong Kong, where a kind of 'velvet fungus' was scraped off the antlers and inscrutably pulverised into a basic ingredient for 'a medicinal or health' product. Any Chinese in drooping health knows what that means, but no herbalist could or would give me the name of the product.

The problem was confused rather than simplified by a half-hearted scientific apologia from one New Zealand exporter, who claimed that the 'velvet' from the antlers was 'quite harmless, and was merely mixed with other ingredients to produce a tasty sauce which compensates for a deficiency in the Chinese diet.' (This theory got a hoarse laugh from bland herbalists in Hong Kong, who know that six babies are born for every person who dies in the colony).

In its trade statistics, the New Zealand Commission in Hong Kong does not specifically identify 'deer antlers' in the Dominion's classification of 'animal products other than meats'. But all products in this category are worth only HK$320,000 a year, so there certainly is not so much reward in deer antlers as in rhinoceros horns.

Discussing this subject, my Hong Kong adviser on Chinese occult affairs, smooth and well-informed, tends to deprecate addiction to 'restorative' powders, blends and beverages. He reckons that a straight shot of snake blood is worth more than a decanter of *ginseng* or a half-serve of Kenya rhinoceros-horn powder. He argues that the elderly — whether natives or visitors to Hong Kong — should concentrate on a special diet. One suggested menu: 'Drunken' shrimps, lobster saute, snapping turtle (preferably with eggs), and roast eels with garlic sauce and aconite. ('Drunken' shrimps are, I guess, an acquired taste. Fresh and alive, they are allowed to kick around a while in a covered bowl of wine, vinegar, ginger and spices. Some skill is needed in handling them, rejecting adroitly the head and tail after administering the *coup de grace* in soy sauce, which, if improperly subdued, they can distribute over your shirt in a death-flurry.)

My adviser did concede that 'an ancient infusion made according to the recipe of a Chinese nobleman' called *King Ning-hualon* — properly 'gold and silver flowers' but irreverently 'sweet and sour flowers' — was a useful standby in emergency.

I asked him what were the ingredients. He patted me kindly on the shoulder. 'Sometimes,' he said, 'it is better not to know.'

Another touted, but cheaper, Hong Kong dish is birds-nest soup, which derives from four varieties of edible nests built by sea swallows inside grottoes along the South China Coast. The varieties, to a connoisseur, differ as sharply as red and white wines, but we needn't go exhaustively into those differences here — save to record that red-tinged nests are supposed to be more nourishing, and are certainly more expensive, than white-grey or green nests. Birds-nest soup is now canned and sometimes poured over noodles — a deviation which depresses a Chinese gourmet as deeply as the mixing of beer and wine in a brandy snifter would agitate a committee member of any wine and food society.

It is a delicate task trying to explain the elements of birds-nest soup to sensitive stomachs. The basic ingredient is bluntly the saliva of the sea swallow, with which the hard-working, low-flying, home-loving birds anoint their fragile houses and fasten them to the rocky ceiling of the grotto. Each nest is about the size of a quartered tennis-ball, just large enough to accommodate the father and mother sea swallow and their inevitable, unvarying, semi-annual brood of two. The father and mother cling to the outside of the nest with outspread wings; the children ferociously demand sustenance indoors.

What do the sea swallows eat? No one is quite sure about the main diet, but it includes moss, seaworms, insects, red ants, spawn from the sea foam and tree sap. The nests are gouged off, or plucked from, the grotto roofs by skilled climbers, scaling bamboo ladders and ropes from skiffs which are tossed around by the tidal waves inside the dark winding caves. Like the young chimney sweeps of Victorian England, agile boys are recruited to squeeze into the crevices and winkle out the nests, which are then cooked and unravelled in boiling water, mixed, decanted and purified for marketing as soup.

Emperor Minh Mang of Vietnam, a vigorous, double-handed trencherman, had a consuming passion for birds-nest soup. Court records insist that, equipped with a large harem, he begot 75 princes and 83 princesses. Considering that he died when he was only twenty (A.D. 1820-40), this should prove something or other — in Hong Kong, Vietnam or anywhere.

THE UNWANTED

They don't call the refugees from the mainland 'White Chinese' these days. That was the name before the bamboo curtain was built and both sides put their armed guards along the frontier. Now those who seek to cross over, either directly into Hong Kong or indirectly through Macao as a staging-post to Hong Kong, run desperate hazards. They are not expatriates; they are escapees.

Not so many enter illegally now: maybe 150 a month, in addition to the approved and screened quota of fifty a day at the border gate of Lowu. And the 'escape routes' through Macao have been virtually closed since Macao capitulated to the demands of Canton in December 1966, and made the bitter agreement to seize and hand back to the Communists any escapees who braved and survived the long night swim and crawled exhausted on to the rocky shores of what was once a sanctuary.

Before the Macao surrender, with its possible portents for Hong Kong, an average of about 400 refugees managed to escape into Macao each month. Most tried to run the gauntlet by boat or by swimming across the dark reaches of the muddy Pearl River estuary, preferably in groups for company and protection. A large but unknown proportion of the swimmers and their home-made floats were swept out to sea, bodies seldom recovered. Regularly, of course, the Communists would push into Macao through the yellow gate at the narrow border groups of blind people, walking in line each with a hand on the shoulder of the man ahead, old people, the lame and the halt, the 'useless mouths'. Macao was never able to pick and choose.

So Macao gradually accumulated a refugee settlement of squatters like Hong Kong's, a colony within a colony, which totals today about 80,000. The young and able-bodied want to get away to Hong Kong, the magnet of glittering opportunity which, Communism or no Communism, would draw venturesome youth from the mainland as New York attracts youth from the mid-west.

Some tried to continue the escape by paying their way as hidden human cargo on junks for the last forty-mile stretch to Hong Kong. The risky trip could cost as high as HK$1,000, which meant that friends or relatives in Hong Kong had put up the money. Others subsisted in Macao, growing their own vegetables, earning a living of sorts by making firecrackers or baskets, accepting charitable handouts. Even those who could earn a living had to 'reside' in Macao for three years before they could move up the long waiting-list to go to guaranteed work in Hong Kong. No one really wanted them — except the Communists, who wanted the return of the young and ablebodied. Their fate among the stranded 80,000 is a matter for grim speculation since Macao has been forced to close the door against future arrivals.

Since the 'cultural revolution', the vanguard of a new class of escapee has been reaching Macao — young technicians, doctors and trained artisans who have grown up under Communist rule, who have been patriotic Chinese with loyalty to the Peking Government, but who did not have the foresight to choose their parents wisely. These parents, it was known, had been 'rich landlords', persons of authority in the Chiang Kai-shek days, upper-middle class families, the evil enemies of the workers. Before the 'cultural revolution', party dogma had assured the children of the Red dawn that, by remorse, application and self-criticism, they could rise above their wicked heritage and decadent instincts and be accepted by the people. But with the advent of the Red Guards, the persecution of the elderly middle class survivors, the looting of their few remaining bourgeois possessions, and the threats to their reclaimed and penitent children, a difficult life appeared to have become a hopeless life. There had not been many of this new type of intelligent, thinking refugee; their escape was doubly precarious because they were the very type which the party cadres could not afford to lose and watched most closely. There will be even fewer now.

Before Macao ceased to be a haven — if only a stopping-place in transit — so-called 'travel agencies' there had managed to organise an underground escape route from China, in collaboration with a ring of recreant officials in China's provincial travel-registration bureaux, who, alas, shared the Macao agencies' fees with all the dexterity and aplomb of corrupt officials under the Manchus.

When I asked some questions about this 'assisted travel service' three years ago, the standard fee for smuggling an elderly Chinese man out of China into Macao was approximately US$ 1500, for an elderly woman $1000. The onward journey to Hong Kong involved an additional charge. If either was conspicuously infirm, crippled, tubercular or otherwise nearing the 'useless-mouth' condition, the prices would fall correspondingly. The liberal-minded officials in the Chinese travel-permit bureaux would have no truck with young and able-bodied travellers, especially technicians, doctors or trained men.

The Macao 'travel agencies' were located at half-a-dozen discreet addresses — now gone with the rising East Wind — near the waterfront. They rejoiced in such mellifluous titles as 'Love-the-Masses Travel Service', 'Honorable Reflections Abroad' and 'Vacations in Happiness and Tranquillity'. They were sometimes bare counters open to the street and set up as make-shift annexes to humble shops selling noodles, firecrackers, sweets, dried fish, soft drinks, charms and Chinese mooncakes. Furnishings consisted of little more than a loyal portrait of Chiang Kai-shek and an out-of-date calendar hanging on the wall behind the counter.

Usually there was not even an attendant on view; the intending patron, after waiting patiently for a few minutes at the counter, withdrew and paced slowly away, knowing that he would be overtaken within a block or two by an impassive travel expert who had apparently sprung from nowhere and who softly inquired what holiday service was desired. (This informal method of business represented laudable respect for the colonial ordinance against the use of official premises in Macao for transactions which could incur the displeasure of the Communist regime.)

One day, in company with a Chinese friend of discretion, I ingenuously inquired the charge for transferring the non-existent father and mother of my cookboy in Hong Kong from an address in suburban Shanghai to Macao. I pictured the father as 65 and the mother as an enfeebled 60. The charge, after bargaining, was US$1,800, as a cut rate, for the pair — plus the rail fare from Shanghai, either 'hard seat' or 'soft seat'. (The cheaper form of travel was objectively recommended as being less likely to attract inconvenient attention to the travellers.)

According to accepted Macao tourist practice, I would be required to pay half the amount down, and the balance on safe arrival of the travellers, who could be expected within a month at the outside. I promised to return. 'We are improving the service,' the agent assured me. 'By next Chinese New Year, we will be able to bring patrons from Shanghai inside three weeks.'

For obvious reasons, no one could make a reliable estimate of the number of Chinese then being smuggled out of the mainland by wealthy or devoted sons and relatives in Macao and Hong Kong. But I ran into my travel agent again that night at the fantan tables in the Central Hotel: clearly a familiar and respected figure, he was changing a thick wad of good American greenbacks.

OPIUM BOOMERANG

There is rich irony — and, the moralist might say, just retribution — in the fact that contemporary Hong Kong's most anxious long-range preoccupation, apart from Peking's inscrutability, is the current smuggling of opium and other drugs into the colony. The wheel has turned. The boomerang has returned. The British colonial authorities are now hag-ridden by the same illicit drug traffic which their free-trade ancestors and prototypes, twelve decades ago, imposed on the hapless Chinese and 'legalised' by war and hypocrisy, 'opening' five treaty ports and grabbing Hong Kong for good measure.

The turn of the wheel would be nicely rounded, and the return of the boomerang exquisitely aimed, if it were the Chinese who were behind the regular flow of opium into the colony. But however dearly the CIA and all enemies of Chinese Communism would like to pinpoint Peking as the master-mind of Asian drug trafficking, there is not a single poppy-petal of evidence to support this theory. The Japanese military used drugs deliberately and systematically to debase the Chinese people during pre-Pearl Harbour days. The Chinese Communists, whatever their other excesses, seem to have shuddered away from drugs, and to have done their best to suppress opium cultivation in Yunnan.

The only Chinese concerned in the long opium trail from the Shan States in Burma, northern Thailand and Laos are, in fact, expatriate Chinese Nationalist Army men, who remained in the hill jungles after Chiang Kai-shek's flight to Formosa, and who have been living off the country ever since. Some of them occasionally cross back over the southern frontiers into China and are reportedly welcomed with open arms, dancing girls and recorded speeches by Chairman Mao. (Although, from all accounts, they might these days find in Szechuan more anti-Mao 'reactionaries' than pro-Mao 'rebels'.)

The smuggled opium is, of course, only the beginning of the drug problem in Hong Kong. The diabolic killer is heroin, a by-product of opium, into which the sweet-smelling poppy-drug is swiftly, expertly and cheaply converted on arrival in Hong Kong from the 'fertile triangle': north-east Burma, northern Thailand and Laos.

These days, when LSD seems to be regarded as an edifying spiritual experience and 'pot' as less harmful than a martini, opium is becoming almost respectable. Opium smoking is illegal in Hong Kong — and now in Macao — but denunciation of heroin is now frequently accompanied by a tolerant shoulder-shrug for its gentle, old-fashioned opium base. However plausible the modern apologia for opium 'smoked within reason', the charges against its heroin derivative are devastating and terrifying. In wine-drinking terms, if opium is supposed to be a light hock, heroin is a mixture of brandy, methylated spirits and cyanide.

The major crime in law-abiding Hong Kong is heroin addiction: sixty percent of the colony's criminals are reckoned to be heroin addicts. More than sixty percent of the colony's prison population of 6,000 have been charged with 'chasing the dragon' — i.e. narcotic offences. It is officially submitted that, of 14,000 addicts who passed through the colony's admirable Tai Lam treatment centre since it was opened in 1958, about forty percent have never been re-convicted. But the number of narcotic offences in which action was taken in 1966 totalled 18,706, compared with 18,341 in 1965. This was the highest category of 'serious crime' in the colony. Two alarming admissions are that heroin addiction is increasing among adolescents, and that Hong Kong has reverted to its old entrepot trade in heroin, and has become a base and distribution point for smuggled export to Japan and the US. An ounce of heroin is worth ten times its Hong Kong price in Yokohama or on the west coast of the USA.

In a recent report on the use of narcotics in Hong Kong, the earnest Reform Club, citing inside sources, estimated that there were at least 100,000 addicts in the colony, compared with 50,000 ten years ago. Authoritative medical opinion is not as reassuring as the Government about cures. Some doctors insist that it is blind folly to argue that re-conviction figures are a reliable measure of rehabilitation and cure, or vice versa.

Nor are statistics available to show how often the sixty percent of re-committed offenders have been re-arrested.

The triad societies are deeply involved in the manufacture of heroin, its local distribution and smuggled export abroad. The Narcotics Bureau police made large seizures of drugs last year, including one coup which netted opium and morphine valued at HK$17 million, shipped into the colony from South East Asia in specially constructed refrigerators. The drug is also concealed in hollowed-out grapefruit, ships' capstans, bags of waste, bamboo stems, false-bottomed crates and other nesting places which would never have occurred to contraband runners along the China coast in the eighties.

As always, there is rumoured to be a local Mr Big behind the Hong Kong traffic in heroin, and sometimes the whispers mention respectable banks and trading firms as active co-agents. But these rumours are inevitable; the only answer to them is that the dedicated members of the Narcotics Bureau, over-worked British and Chinese alike, who know at first hand the effects of heroin, would secrete a bomb under the Hong Kong Club or the Cricket Club if the explosion would blast a masked master-mind into the open. They work, of course, closely with informers — the *ma chai*, or 'little horses', as they are called.

Today's Opium Trail to Hong Kong is more complicated and hazardous than the old clipper route from Calcutta and Bombay, past Macao, to Lintin Island, and then via the Pearl River backwaters that by-passed Canton. Now the trail follows either the 2,600-mile course of the Mekong River to Phnom Penh (Cambodia's under-policed capital), or along jungle trails, first openly to Chiengmai (northern Thailand), and then by pre-arrangement to Bangkok. According to the UN, opium production in South East Asia from the charming *papaver somniferum*, or white poppy, totalled 1,000 million metric tons in 1966, of which four-fifths was grown in Burma. The old opium routes — Rangoon, Bangkok and Saigon in the late 1940's and the direct unashamed route via Bangkok until 1957

— have now perforce been abandoned since the Vietnam war and the outlawing of opium in Bangkok.

Traffic along the new Opium Trail, which finally ends in Hong Kong, is beset by lively adventures and bitter 'private wars'. There are frequent reports of armed clashes and ambushes between rival groups of Burmese and Chinese Nationalist traffickers, seeking to defend or high-jack each other's caravans or river-borne flotillas.

You can still smoke opium openly in Chiengmai, Phnom Penh, and any town in Laos or northern Burma, but not in Bangkok or Saigon — nor, of course, in Hong Kong. The casual, curious smoker of opium, it is true, comes to little harm; the compulsive opium smoker would probably have become an alcoholic had he been a Westerner.

I had my own first opium in Shanghai in 1940, with respectable *taipans* who smoked three or four pipes in a depressingly non-mysterious divan off Nanking Road every Friday afternoon. I had my last opium in Bangkok with a Siamese doctor friend on the eve of Prime Minister Sarit's abolition of the national sport. I found it singularly overrated: no dreams, only a heightened sense of colour and psychic and physical self-esteem, with a loss of interest in the passing of the hours and the passing of women — altogether unrewarding.

But heroin is something vastly and appallingly different. It is Hong Kong's number one internal problem in all crime and violence, and one for which Chairman Mao and his imponderable external policies and plots cannot be blamed.

There cannot be heroin without opium. One wonders what the original respectable opium runners would have had to say today. It is quite likely that in the mid-1800's they had never heard of a boomerang.

CHINA WATCHERS

Every Far Eastern foreign reporter of the Chinese scene, diplomat or pressman, is a China watcher, whether he operates, frustrated and isolated, on the spot in Peking, or, frustrated and peering, from a distance in Hong Kong. Whichever his base, he cannot be a participant of the scene as, for instance, an English, French or Australian reporter can be in Washington. Even if he is a Communist, he is still doomed to be only a watcher because he is not Chinese.

It is of course impossible to write satisfactorily or satisfyingly about a country which you have never seen (Arthur Waley was the prodigious exception that tests this rule). But a plausible argument can be sustained that, over a period, China watchers in Hong Kong, who have at one time known the Chinese scene and people at first hand, can operate more freely, fully, rewardingly and objectively than their counterparts who are allowed to set up their telescopes and typewriters inside Peking.

Information from and about China droppeth like the heavy rain from heaven upon the Hong Kong watcher beneath, but flooding and oft confusing, rather than blessing, him that takes. There are swift and efficient daily translations from the Chinese newspapers which are allowed to enter Hong Kong — plus many provincial papers which arrive surreptitiously; all Chinese internal radio news services are monitored and translated with equal rapidity; official pronouncements and party and government releases are known in Hong Kong as soon as in Peking; the skilled staff of the US consulate-general — larger than most US embassies — translates and distributes without opinion or comment the contents of the Chinese press; an expert and highly specialised British information service is available; and authorities like Union Research (conducted by Chinese scholars and subsidised by the US), the multi-racial University Service Centre (Carnegie Foundation), and Father La Dany's weekly *China News Analysis* promulgate learned reasoning, discoveries and opinion which would be rank heresy inside Peking.

There are also six Chinese Communist papers in Hong Kong, two of which are party megaphones, whose astonishing fabrications and aberrations are in themselves an indirect guide to party policy.

A China watcher absent from base for a couple of weeks finds his telescope buried beneath masses of translations, magazines, pamphlets, mimeographed reports, handouts and extracts from Chairman Mao's published wit and wisdom.

The reporter in Peking can get unofficial but vital human news, as in any strange city, from the faces of the people, the restaurant menus, the manner of the police and the contents and prices in shop windows. But he can never win access openly to policy-makers or privately to policy-critics. His copy is not censored (although some sensitive telegraphists in Peking refused to transmit some Red Guard *graffiti* at the height of the 'cultural revolution') but he can be carpeted by insolent Foreign Office party mandarins and warned that his messages are disapproved. (On the other hand, I was once called back, after lodging a news message in Peking, and congratulated formally by the pig-tailed little girl who took the cables for my 'very neatly typed and very clear message'.)

The two Western resident agencies — Reuters and Agence France Presse — know very well that it is wiser not to press controversial, on-the-spot news inquiries with reckless crusading zeal. When I was first reporting out of Communist China in 1956-57, at the time of Chairman Mao's 'hundred flowers' confidence trick, Jacques Locquain of AFP lived in a Chinese house in a *hutung* (lane) near the famed 'Three Tables' restaurant, rode a bicycle like the locals and held nominal office in his local neighbourhood association. David Chipp, his youthful Reuter opposition, laboured night and day in a room in the Hsinchiao Hotel near the Gate of Heavenly Peace. They had different contacts and they exploited all local news prospects with enterprise, diligence and intelligence. But neither, to my recollection, ever scored a beat over the other because they were honest reporters and factual interpreters, and their different sources were equally restricted — like those of their frustrated resident counterparts today.

Whenever they were summoned to a Government department for an important Peking handout, they did not even then have an advantage over China watchers in distant Hong Kong, because the New China News Agency had simultaneously broadcast the handout to the world.

Most experienced China watchers agree that the ideal way to cover China in its present travail would be to select two good hard newsmen, who had done their Chinese homework properly and who maintained reliable files, and to appoint one to Hong Kong and one to Peking, interchanging them every six months. This arrangement would merge the perspective and freedom of Hong Kong news coverage with the spot observation and artificial authority of the Peking dateline, and, by allowing the Peking man to emerge regularly for fresh air in Hong Kong, would help to quarantine his natural revulsion against an unnatural society.

China watchers in Hong Kong have another advantage over those in Peking: Chinese refugees talk with abandon, if often anonymously, about the conditions which they have escaped. With the benefit of honourable hindsight, it is now clear that we China watchers in Hong Kong were too suspicious of the stories of bitter resentment and repression which we were hearing from refugees in early 1965, and which heralded the 'great proletarian cultural revolution'. They sounded too much like Chiang Kai-shek propaganda.

A sincere China watcher must read—or at least skim—every magazine that comes out of China, from *China Reconstructs* to *Women of China*. He must study every formal list of office holders. He must read the fine-print footnotes to abstruse and turgid articles in Red egghead publications with enticing titles like *Planning and Statistics* and *Philosophic Research*. He must never ignore a round-up of official guests at a banquet for delegates from an Albanian collective farm or an African cultural troupe. He is like the sincere Sussex bird-watcher who unfailingly counts all the sparrows as they pass because he knows that, on one magnificent day of revelation, they will escort, even if partly hidden, the first red-rumped tit from Iceland ever to be seen in an English autumn.

Peking party protocol is as shattering as the edicts of the Imperial Dragon in the Forbidden City when lesser Maos were Emperors. A change in place of an honoured party name at table or in the reviewing stand at the Gate of Heavenly Peace is often the first evidence of promotion or a heavy fall downstairs. The first indication of the unlikely promotion of Madam Mao Tse-tung, the original and only Communist starlet to marry the producer and to try to take over the production, was the appearance of her maiden name Chiang Ching — which was a tricky one for incautious China watchers — in the list of top party brass welcoming the 'little generals' of the Red Guards.

GHOST OF FU MANCHU

The tong, triad or Chinese secret society persists wherever Chinese live and however distant their expatriate homes are from China. Not even the Communists have eradicated triads in Canton or Shanghai, and, with respectable Chinese friends, I have met loyal members of the celebrated '14-K' triad in Djakarta, Singapore, San Francisco's Chinatown and even Melbourne's Little Bourke Street. Nor have the British in Hong Kong or the Chinese Nationalists in Formosa succeeded in suppressing the criminal type of triads.

Originally, like the Society of Harmonious Fists, which launched the Boxers against the foreign devils in Peking, the secret societies or triads were blood brotherhoods, with Oriental Masonic undertones, which were pledged to self-protection, moral ideals and even semi-religious principles. Their history is supposed to go back to AD 1700, when five Buddhist monks of implausible martial ability, called the First Five Ancestors, organised the Hung Family to defend the Ming dynasty against the Manchus. The '14-K' triad was resurrected and rejuvenated in Canton, in the late 1930's, by the redoubtable Nationalist General Koi Sui-heong, who used it as a secret information agency for the Kuomintang.

In 1949, the general found sanctuary in Hong Kong — as Chou En-lai and Ho Chi-minh had done in different circumstances and for different reasons — and set about organising eighteen sub-branches of the '14-K' as a nucleus of secret agents and saboteurs to facilitate eventual Nationalist return to China. His legacy lingers.

The '14-K' got its name from its old honourable address at number 14 in Po-wah Road, Canton; the 'K' was added to signify 'karat' of gold, after the upstart members of a rival tong, who proclaimed the superior virtues of softer non-karat local gold, were cut to pieces with knives and swords in a democratic street head-count.

In those more leisurely days, formal initiation ceremonies into the '14-K' lasted throughout the night — 'worse than our elevation to the thirty-third degree,' as an irreverent Masonic friend once told me. Before smouldering joss-sticks on a Buddhist-style altar, the candidates swore no fewer than thirty-six life-and-death oaths, and drank from deep bowls of wine, cinnabar, rooster's blood, and a drop or two of blood from their own fingers. They also bowed to the Ten Precious Articles, which included a red lamp (distinguishing the true from the false), a white paper fan (which strikes down all traitors), and a sword of peach-wood (which can decapitate enemies when merely flourished in the air). And finally they cast their joss-sticks to the floor with the solemn request that their own lives be similarly extinguished if they were untrue to their pledges or unfaithful to their brothers. Picturesque death penalties ranged from the orthodox 'ten thousand knife cuts' to the haunting 'exposure to thunderclaps'.

Like all pageantry and ceremonial in this frantic modern world, triad initiation in Hong Kong has now been debased to a perfunctory exchange of finger-pricking in a hillside squatter's hut or a slum cockloft. In the same way, Masonic-like aspirations have degenerated into Mafia-like extortion, racketeering, blackmail and terrorism. The '14-K' in Hong Kong has lost its lofty ideals, also its spiritual cohesion. So have other secret tongs with names which Confucius and Lao-tse would have approved: the Alliance Society, the Flood Gate of Mercy, and the United Benevolent Society. Nominal triad membership is supposed to be still around 200,000, although the colony's police insist that active and dangerous members total only 10,000 who are split into rival groups, and whose 'stand-over' persecution could be swiftly broken if their victims — passive members or non-members — would only call their bluff and name them to the police. But Hong Kong, one keeps repeating, is China, and many Chinese still fear the traditions and threats of the triads more than they trust the assurances of British police.

So the triads, hollow and divided, continue to 'protect' and promote the drug traffic, juvenile prostitution and illicit gambling in the colony. They are always waiting eagerly to organise violence and rioting, arson and looting, whenever there are demonstrations or disturbances in the colony. They are the Communists' best ally in Hong Kong. Also their influence and 'squeeze' strengthens the cynical conviction among most Chinese that there is widespread corruption in the police force.

The triad bosses no longer carry the old symbolic marked coin or cotton badge, but, like the old, all-powerful 'Greens' in Shanghai of the thirties and forties, they can identify themselves to lowly members by the way they light or hold a cigarette, push a teacup to a waiter, or wave a greeting in the street.

The 'Greens' bossed the Shanghai underworld until the Pacific war, and maintained an iron discipline and dread authority which the Hong Kong triads, in their wildest moments, have never pretended to wield. They had a million retainers in the Yangtze valley, and probably 100,000 members in Shanghai. They dealt directly but discreetly with the French police in Frenchtown, who welcomed their cooperation in solving crimes in which the 'Greens' had had no financial or 'protection' interest. The two head men were Dou Fu-seng and Wang Hsiao-lai, who managed to live Jekyll-and-Hyde lives, combining banking, commercial and municipal interests with their careers of terror, extortion and murder.

In their Hyde roles, Dou was the 'organisation' man of the 'Greens'; Wang looked after the finances. In their Jekyll roles, Dou was president of the Chung Wai and Tung Wai banks and director of the Greet China University and the China Merchants' Steam Navigation Company; Wang was chairman of the Provisional Government of Greater Shanghai and chairman of the Chinese Chamber of Commerce. Chiang Kai-shek was in their debt; they assisted him in the massacre of Communists in 1927.

(Dou overcame the opium habit, which had been slowly killing him. I saw Wang once at the French Club in 1940. He was a hulking yellow nightmare of a man with a pock-marked face and was known as 'Small-pox' or 'Million-Dollar' Wang. It is regrettable that no one has ever written their biographies.)

Compared with the Shanghai 'Greens', today's vicious Hong Kong triads are a poor and empty lot, but it would be a mistake to belittle them and their influence. They were able to inflame and exploit the disastrous riots of 1956, which led to martial law. They touched off the looting after the Kowloon demonstrations against the proposed ferry-fare increase in 1966. They moved gladly into the Communist-instigated rioting in 1967, when the comrades, having overplayed their hand, sullenly retreated to try to dig in. On hire, they made and threw bombs for the party. They represent, in fact, a hidden Chinese weapon, ready for non-ideological response to any future Communist violence. By accident and the force of circumstances, they would be as useful to the Communists in Hong Kong in the future as the 'Greens', by design and pay-off, were to Chiang Kai-shek in 1927 Shanghai.

Because of their association with the heroin and drug traffic generally, the Hong Kong triads have already been partly responsible for involving the colony's government diplomatically with Peking over, of all things, the pest-hole of slums, filth and disease, rats and vice, in Kowloon known as the Walled City (it is neither walled nor a city). It is the worst slum area in the colony and should be razed. However, it is alleged to be technically under Peking's jurisdiction because of some lawyer's loophole in the old treaty with China. Triad gangsters have their headquarters in this cesspool and, whenever the Government moves to replace an outer section of the stinking hovels, they unite with the Communists in denouncing British colonial trespass on Chinese sovereignty. In this concocted cause, one can only say that each of the Communist and triad protagonists is worthy of his ally.

A Chinese underworld pattern in reverse thus repeats itself as the Hong Kong triads emerge as minor but dangerous jackals for the Communists, just as their far tougher Shanghai prototypes, the 'Greens', helped in the task of suppressing the Communists in Shanghai two decades ago.

Like the ghost of Fu Manchu, this Chinese triad tradition cannot be laid. As a glum historical footnote, it should be recorded that the triads pestered the first colonial administration of Hong Kong, which issued an abortive ordinance in 1845 'to Suppress the Triads and other Secret Societies, which Associations have Objects in View which are incompatible with the Maintenance of Good Order and constituted Authority, and with the Security of Life and Property, and afford, by Means of a secret Agency, increased Facilities for the Commission of Crime and for the Escape of Offenders.'

SUZIE WONG, ETCETERA

The Luk Kwok Hotel, the original of Richard Mason's waterfront bordello, Nam Kwok, in *The World of Suzie Wong,* has been respectabilised. The once crowded ground-floor, juke-box dance-hall is now a dull and empty desert of tea-tables surrounded, in the neighbouring Wanchai streets, by oases of phoney 'Suzie Wong' bars and pick-up joints, with beer-puddled cubicles and slit-skirted hostesses where the shyest of men can find a girl or a broken nose with the greatest of ease. To the young in heart or the sailor in a hurry, they are, I suppose, havens of a sort, although terribly sleazy but just as expensive when compared with their elegant prototypes in Tokyo's Ginza, Shibuya and Shinjuku areas.

In the Luk Kwok, the slow old elevators, with their open ornamental Parisian-style grillwork, still groan and clank as they anchor uncertainly at the residential floors, but they now carry elderly tourists and their wives instead of the cage-loads of twittering Suzie Wongs and sailor patrons of five years ago. There is a plaque in the old dance-hall which recalls its faded days — and nights — of glory. But today's roisterers, sailors, soldiers and lonely men find their poor grog and sad pleasure elsewhere, either in the Wanchai and Causeway Bay tenderloin areas on 'Hong Kong side' or in the pimp-crowded Kowloon streets, illuminated with neon signs which are not as dazzling and futuristic as the Ginza's (and which, by stern colonial law, cannot blink or move) but which light the wayfarer's eager or faltering steps to open house and open palms until 2 a.m., instead of Tokyo's midnight curfew.

There are fewer than 200 licensed bars and 100 licensed dance-halls in Hong Kong, but because they are concentrated in a glittering, neon orgasm, the visitor gets the impression that there must be far more. No one knows the number of call-girls (or 'family girls', as the curious Hong Kong jargon goes), dance hostesses, bar-girls and plain whores in the colony, but, as an

Asian port, 'rest and recuperation centre', military garrison town, and jumping tourist centre, Hong Kong faces up adequately and uncomplainingly to its carnal responsibilities. Street-walking is restricted. Otherwise night life is wide open, if not as blatant as in, say, Bangkok, where all taxi-drivers labour under the respectful delusion that every Western visitor is in panting search, all round the clock, for girls, boys, massage, exhibitions and blue movies, literally from one breakfast to the next.

Prostitution was legal in Hong Kong until 1932. Tai-Ping-Shan — today's Cat Street area, where earnest tourists sniff stale opium and scratch for dusty bargains — was the colony's first red-light district. But it was an unlovely area and no place for gentlemen. Not until the celebrated Madam Randall, heading a theatrical troupe from Australia, arrived in 1851 and appraised the scene, did Hong Kong get the bordello set-up it deserved; the colony's vice then lost half its evil by losing all its grossness.

Madam Randall quit the stage and became Hong Kong's first real madam. She had the same instincts for business with refinement as Mistress Kate Townsend revealed at number 40 Basin Street, New Orleans, ten years later. Her first house was a discreet establishment in Lyndhurst Terrace; her girls were hand picked for charm as well as beauty; the furnishings of the rooms reflected full-blown Victorian taste; introductions were effected with a flourish in a luxurious drawing-room which reminded many lonely expatriates of home. It was a tricky task to begin advertising her business in the public prints, but Madam Randall adopted a formula which amused her patrons:

HONEY

At Mrs Randall's — a small quantity of Good HONEY in small jars; also GIN, BRANDY, SHERRY, PORT, CHAMPAGNE, CLARET, BOTTLED BEER, PORTER, etc. etc.

Lyndhurst Terrace,
Victoria, 12th June, 1851.

The normal run of Hong Kong's addresses of convenience
and dingy hotel rooms today lack the velvet amenities of the
Lyndhurst Terrace apiary, although there were once whispers
of tolerated halls of mirrors and mechanical beds in North Point
— Hong Kong's 'little Shanghai'. Now apartments and 'family
girls' have taken over.

At the waterfront bars and dance-halls, the girls toss down
the customary 'chelly blandy' or other fake liquor and must be
'bought out' for thirty or fifty dollars to accompany a suitor
to another address, where the boss pimp takes up to forty percent
or more of the girl's earnings. The prettiest girls and the best
bands are at several ballrooms which have no liquor licences, and
where refreshments are restricted to soft drinks, hot tea and
melon seeds. These are usually favoured by well-to-do Chinese;
visitors in uniform are unwelcome; and some of the girls, like
top Kyoto *geisha*, are 'protected' by patrons who cannot yet
afford concubines. Of the available dance hostesses, there are
many who are not prostitutes but whose glittering dress and
sophisticated manners often persuade foreigners to 'buy them
out' for respectable but attractive company at dinner or a ca-
baret.

For the adventurous or the romantic with a love of the sea,
small sampans at Causeway Bay or Aberdeen operate a humble
version of the *fahteng* — those friendly flower-boats of old Canton
which Chairman Mao's puritanical cadres have sunk without
trace. These sampans, with companion, can be hired for about
ten Hong Kong dollars an hour or thirty dollars for the night.
They drift like ungainly gondolas with the tide and pick up
noodles, tea and beer from floating restaurants and even alfresco
serenades from rafts of drunken musicians. Modesty is ensured
by a curtain which conceals the two passengers from the bored
boatman. For aromatic reasons, the sensitive sniff the tide

before setting out for romance at sea.

Hong Kong, characteristically, encourages an unofficial but effective colonial system of surveillance over commercialised sex. Proprietors of many dance-halls and bars, who don't want to have their social centres put 'off-limits' by military police or shore patrols, cooperate with the Medical and Health Department and issue 'Blue Cards', which actually are white, to their girls, who must have them 'chopped' each week at clinics. Like so many operations in Hong Kong, the practice is individualistic and haphazard, and depends on a voluntary, mutually rewarding partnership between authority and capitalist enterprise. It is, however, surprisingly effective.

There are areas of contradiction in which regulations mix up white cards with red tape. For instance, one clutch of regulations says that no girls under eighteen can be employed in dance-halls, but another set permits girls between the ages of fourteen and eighteen to work in 'bars.'

* * *

Until 1967 the British colonial government in Hong Kong accepted the ancient Chinese law or custom which classified concubines as legal wives. A new regulation — introduced with proper British phlegm and irrelevance during the crisis of the May riots — revokes this immemorial sanction which the Communists naturally outlawed fourteen years ago. British surrender to internal pressure by elderly unmarried Chinese suffragettes and straight-laced public servants, it must be stressed, was welcomed by few of those number one Chinese wives in Hong Kong who placidly and realistically approved their husband's choice of a number two, number three and even number four wife.

The Chinese do not use the brutal word 'concubine'. They prefer the light, rather charming word *tsip* (pronounced something like 'tea-sip'). The number one legal wife — some of my Chinese and Japanese friends, having the customary Oriental difficulty over pronouncing *l*, say and sometimes write 'regal' wife — is known as the *tsai*.

The modern *tsai*, as the ruler of a perfectly respectable and harmonious harem, knew always that she was in control of the household. Asian wives are far more sensible, mature and assured than Western wives about the facts of married life. Many Chinese wives in Hong Kong prefer that their husbands take other 'wives.' A Chinese husband who has several wives is clearly a successful man, like a Western husband with several motor cars. It is another way of keeping up with the Wongs. A Chinese *tsai* gains face by indulging one or several secondary 'wives'.

An instructive aside here is that it will usually be discovered that the *tsai* had an unfortunate habit of bearing daughters.

'Naturally I would hope that my husband, who works too hard at the office, kept his *tsips* here at our home, rather than in separate establishments which can become very expensive,' one charming and respectable Chinese wife once told me. 'Besides, they might then be unknown to me. Why, I introduced my husband's second *tsip* to him. A lovely stupid girl. He likes her now much better than the first *tsip*, whom he selected himself. He is a very intelligent man, but he needs a wife's guidance. Men are often so helpless in domestic matters'.

In the happier Hong Kong days which are now ended, there was no formal ceremony for a 'marriage' with a *tsip*. When a *tsai* received a *tsip* into the house and the *tsip* served her tea, the union was established and legally binding. This flexibility has been abolished by the Government's new ordinance.

'We are as bad as the Communists now,' a Hong Kong tycoon of Rotarian eminence complained to me when the British colonial 'reform' became law. 'Britain's so-called "morality" laws would appeal more to Chairman Mao than to happy Chinese here who have never surrendered their traditional links with the fatherland however temporarily occupied and despoiled by the Communists. Surely we Chinese can arrange our private lives better than any foreign Government can do by wishful bureaucratic interference.'

This pillar of conservatism, who may well be knighted next year by a grateful British sovereign, is generous, charitable and law-abiding. He is the father of two daughters by his *tsai*, a son by one *tsip,* and a daughter by his second *tsip*. All these children are legitimate under the old Chinese law and, if the father dies intestate (which, I am assured, very few Chinese fathers do), all will be entitled to share his inheritance equally.

It was recalled, by those Hong Kong Chinese who deplored the end of concubinage, that, when the 'reform' was originally mooted in the colony fourteen years ago, Hong Kong's most revered Chinese lawyer, Sir Man Kam Lo, successfully submitted that polygamy was sanctioned by 'immemorial Chinese law', and had been preserved by the colony's founding charter of 1843 and had received the highest judicial approval.

I remember a realistic exchange between husband and *tsai* in the presence of a couple of gay but subservient *tsips* when, first arriving in Hong Kong, I was young and presumptuous enough to probe the difficulties and advantages of concubinage.

'It is often more convenient,' said the *tsai*. 'Sometimes I don't feel like going to a dance or a night-club or the theatre. So my husband can take one of the *tsips*.'

'Or even the two of them,' the husband remarked incautiously.

'Or even the three of us, if I should change my mind,' she interposed.

'Of course, of course,' the husband agreed hastily.

An interesting segregationist by-product of the repeal of the century-old Chinese Marriage Preservation Ordinance in Hong Kong was the correlated abolition of the anomaly under which it was technically an offence for a Chinese man to commit adultery with a Chinese married woman but not with a married non-Chinese woman. Nor had it been an offence in the colony for a non-Chinese man to commit adultery with a Chinese married woman.

*   *   *

ITEM: Of the 92,476 live births in Hong Kong in 1966, only 67 were registered as illegitimate and lacked the name of the father in the birth entry.

*   *   *

I have had the honour of escorting Ian Fleming, on his only visit to Hong Kong, and my employer, Lord Thomson, on his first visit, to the old Luk Kwok — on each occasion, I hasten needlessly to add, purely in a mood of curiosity and investigation.

Each time business was dull and some of the 'family girls' were knitting, while the huge golden juke-box bellowed and shook.

Ian took a reporter's interest in the signs: 'Girls, But No Obligation To Buy Drinks! Clean Surroundings! Take It Easy! You Are At Home! Fine Food And Wines! Enjoy To The Maximum At The Least Expenses!' But he seemed to be more taken with the Siamese fighting-fish in the huge bowl than with the Suzie Wongs in their small cubicles.

Lord Thomson's reactions were also typical. I thought we looked a respectable pair of visitors, mature, personable and substantial, although perhaps a shade too Rotarian. So when two girls swooped down beside us, I explained that we were a couple of pay-master sergeants off the US carrier which had just berthed from Honolulu. Lord Thomson, without flicking an eyelash, nodded solemnly and sipped his beer with a nautical air. One girl addressed us both in excellent and grateful English: 'Thank you, dears. We like it better when you boys come here not wearing uniform.'

During the ensuing desultory conversation, Lord Thomson

carefully studied the prices of the drinks on the menu and made a few notes on an envelope. He then — somewhat to my surprise — asked his companion: 'How much to go upstairs?' 'Thirty dollars for an hour, dear, plus ten dollars for the room,' she replied, hope lighting her soft eyes. Lord Thomson made another note. 'How much is the rent for a single room unaccompanied?' he next inquired. 'Twenty dollars,' — and perplexity replaced hope in her eyes. Lord Thomson nodded thoughtfully and jotted down another figure.

We tipped the girls generously and they bowed us to the door, where the Thomson limousine waited to whisk the paymaster sergeants back to Fenwick Pier and the anchored carrier.

'Why the questions?' I asked. 'You're not thinking of buying the place, are you?'

'No,' he replied absently, then reflected and added: 'But I could do worse, don't you think?'

I have never seen the influence of Hong Kong work so swiftly on a man so obviously cut out to be a *taipan*.

Hong Kong Yesterday

GOVERNOR WITHOUT A SHIRT

Hong Kong did not exist, so it was necessary to invent it. Though involuntary, the process of invention was logical enough, but everyone involved, willingly or reluctantly, was denounced and punished. On the British side (the winners), the honest man personally responsible, Trade Superintendent Captain Charles Elliot, RN, was sacked for bad judgment with good intentions, and ended up in exile, first as Consul-General to Texas, and then as Governor of St Helena (an instructive order in priorities today). On the Chinese side (the losers), the honest man personally responsible, High Commissioner Lin Tse-hsu, and the dishonest man personally responsible, High Commissioner Kishen, were sacked for bad judgment with bad intentions, and banished respectively to Siberia and Tibet.

Kishen and Elliot, in later years, remembered each other with compassion and respect. 'Poor devil,' said Elliot of Kishen on St Helena. 'I suppose the Emperor beheaded him.' — 'Elliot was an honest man,' said Kishen in Lhasa. 'I hear that Queen Victoria beheaded him.'

Young Queen Victoria wrote: '*All* we wanted might have been got if it had not been for the unaccountably strange conduct of Chas. Elliot. . . . He tried to obtain the *lowest* terms from the Chinese.' Viscount Palmerston, Foreign Secretary, wrote to Elliot: 'You have disobeyed and neglected your Instructions; you have deliberately abstained from employing the *Force* placed at your disposal; and you have without sufficient necessity accepted Terms which fall far short of those you were instructed to obtain. . . . You have obtained the cession of Hong Kong, a bare Island with hardly a House upon it. Now it seems obvious that Hong Kong will not be a Mart of Trade, any more than Macao is so.'

The Imperial Dragon, thoughtfully appropriating Kishen's ten million pounds' worth of personal property and wealth, wrote with his vermilion brush: 'After Kishen arrived in Canton, he willingly succumbed to the wiles of the rebel Barbarians. . . Hong Kong is an important place. How could the said Kishen allow the rebels to occupy it officially? A misdemeanor so high shows indeed that he has no conscience. Let him be deprived of his post and imprisoned.'

The whole tragi-comic charade which precipitated the first war between England and China — exactly one century before the Second World War — was the result of misunderstanding and mutual ignorance between the East and West. The misunderstanding and ignorance persist. Chairman Mao Tse-tung probably knows less about the Western world today than Emperor Tao Kuang did a century and a half ago.

Even the gods seemed to frown on Hong Kong's birth. Within a month of the first land-sale on the island (June 1841), a typhoon unroofed every new building on the waterfront, rumbled away into China, and then, unappeased, roared back within a week to destroy all repair work. The only structures to escape ruin, the morbid noted, were the Matheson Opium House and the Chinese cemetery.

For good measure, the founder of the colony, Captain Elliot, still unaware that he had been disgraced by Palmerston, was caught and shipwrecked in the same typhoon on the rocky islands of the Ladrones (the Robbers), in the Pearl River estuary, and was rescued by Chinese fishermen who carried him to Macao, 'wearing only a Manila hat, jacket and striped trousers, but no shirt'.

DOUBLE FAILURE

The British had made two high-level attempts to interest the Lord of the World, the Dispenser of Light from the Court of Heaven, and the Imperial Dragon in opening China to trade with the West. The attempts were so futile that they hardly bear thinking about.

Milord Macartney went to Peking in 1793. He urbanely evaded the kowtow ceremony (crawling on hands and knees and bumping the head nine times on the ground in front of the Dragon) by insisting that a mandarin of his rank should perform the same ceremony before a painting of George III, which he had brought with him; and had breakfast with the Dragon, who gave him a specimen of his handwriting, the Imperial run-around and a sharp knock-back: 'We possess all things in abundance and have no need of the manufactures of outside Barbarians'.

Milord Amherst arrived a couple of decades later, after Waterloo, and suffered an even more humiliating experience. He carried no portrait of the British monarch and might indeed have kowtowed had the Great Chamberlain not overplayed his hand and tried to rush him into a dawn audience with the Dragon before His Lordship had shaved or changed his linen after a rough all-night journey by sedan chair to the Summer Palace. He bucked at the court mandarin's precipitance, and the Great Chamberlain told the Dragon that His Lordship was laid low with a stomach ache, as also, the Great Chamberlain insisted, were his deputies. So the embassy was ordered to leave China.

The Amherst mission accomplished only one distinction: it put Hong Kong on the map, if obscurely, by secretly picking up a British and an American interpreter, who were *persona non grata* in Canton, at a rendezvous off the west coast of the island en route to Peking. This seems to have been the first recorded British reference to Hong Kong.

Appropriately, the Amherst mission was shipwrecked on the way home and had to be content with seeing Napoleon on St Helena instead of the Dragon in Peking.

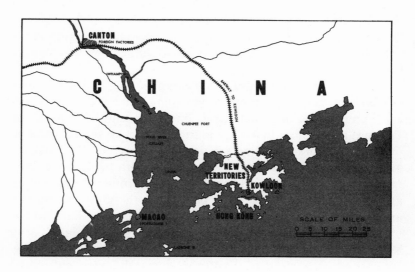

FOREIGN MUD

'Foreign mud,' as the Chinese officials called opium, had become the illegal basis for regulated British trade with China through Canton, where the East India Company had set up humble house in 1715. One or two points should be clarified here. The British did not force opium on the Chinese, who grew few poppies themselves when they picked up a liking for the pipe from the Javanese Dutch through Formosa. Chinese demand always exceeded foreign supply at the curious foreign settlement which the Chinese tolerated on the Canton waterfront, and at the numerous ports along the China coast which the opium-runners regularly visited.

Contraband opium, which the Chinese Emperor had banned, was the only way in which the foreign devils could make the Chinese trade return a worthwhile profit. They had to pay in silver for the tea, silk and rhubarb which they bought from China. The Chinese bought in return some cotton goods, although they sniffed at woollens, but British trade was floundering deeply in the red until smuggled opium from Bengal began to divert the flow of silver from east to west. The East India Company, which had a monopoly of British trade in the Orient, followed the Portuguese example and began to smuggle opium through corrupt mandarins and officials and the closed shop of the Cantonese merchants known as the Hong.

Macao, the Portuguese settlement, and Hong Kong, the British colony, are perched on the western and eastern approaches respectively to the twenty-mile wide estuary of the Pearl River. The island Lintin ('Solitary Nail'), a 2,000-foot peak about twenty miles up the brown river-bay, was the public but unofficial centre of opium smuggling in the Canton area. Here the 'foreign mud' was discharged from the Indiamen and the clippers into open barges which carried the contraband, then in the care of the Chinese buyers, up the maze of waterways that led to Canton, another fifty miles upstream. The trade openly conducted at the thirteen 'factories', or foreign settlement, in Canton was technically illegal, although much of the actual buying and selling of the opium was conducted by the foreign devils at this settlement outside the walls of Canton. The approach to the port-city was through a winding rocky defile, known as the Bogue, and guarded by forts and bristling batteries of cannon which the British overran and seized with the greatest ease when war broke out.

Life in the thirteen factories, which were really combined warehouses, dormitories and living quarters, was subject to severe restrictions imposed by the Chinese Viceroy, the Governor

of Canton and the Court official known as the Hai Kwan Pu,
an honourable title which was rendered as the Hoppo in pidgin.
The Hoppo 'squeezed' the Hong managers who conducted trade
with the foreign devils, and who 'squeezed' them in term. The
Viceroy and the Governor 'squeezed' the Hoppo, and the Emperor 'squeezed' the Viceroy and the Governor. It was a
perfectly straightforward arrangement, organised on traditional
Chinese lines.

Although the opium transactions were handled openly,
the foreign devils did not unload opium without disguise on to
the wharves outside their factories. Occasionally some wretched
coolies on the hulks or barges which brought most of the foreign
mud upstream were arrested and strangled for their crime, but
this action was taken only when reports from Peking suggested
that the Lord of Ten Thousand Years would like some assurance
and evidence that the opium traffic was being properly policed.
There were also diverting scenes downstream at the mouth of
the Pearl River where Chinese armed junks would sometimes
put on a good show of pursuing a foreign clipper after it had
discharged its opium at Lintin, loaded its tea and silk and
rhubarb, and was putting to sea. For dramatic effect, they
would fire their cannon at the foreign vessel when it was safely
out of range, and the Chinese captains would then file their
reports about a successful encounter with a marauding barbarian
who had been put to flight when he sought to smuggle opium.
These reports made reassuring reading in the Summer Palace
or the Forbidden City, six weeks away by river-canal post.

There were as many as 150 British residents at one time in
the Canton settlement, and there were also Dutch, Danish,
Spanish, French, American and Parsee representatives in their
national buildings. The East India Company paid £20,000
a year rental for its warehouse, or the equivalent of, say, one
hundred chests of good Bengal opium. The Yankees had been
late arrivals, but proved to be sharp, smart and ingratiating
operators. The British thought they were a shade too deferential

to the Hong traders and the Hoppo. Also they sold Smyrna opium, which most traders agreed was a poor show because Smyrna opium was definitely inferior to the Indian product and some scrupulous traders feared that it might be harmful to health.

Regulations insisted that the foreign devils could not bring wives or women into the factories, possess weapons, hire their own servants, enter Canton city or remain in the factories during the summer months, when they retreated to Macao. Their ships had to discharge and load at Whampoa, thirteen miles downstream. They could enjoy three visits each month out of their enclosure to public gardens on a nearby island, but were not permitted to travel in groups of more than ten, or to get drunk, or to stay out after dark. And, as we have seen, all smuggling was absolutely forbidden.

However, the foreign devils seemed to get on comfortably enough. Their personal contacts among the Hong merchants were friendly and understanding, and it is surmised that young women, who definitely were not available on the flower-boats or floating brothels on the river, probably dropped in discreetly from time to time to share a cup of tea, which naturally was always stored in abundance in the factories. The foreigners ate well and their wine cellars were always well stocked with deliveries from Macao.

HOG LANE

The foreign ships often had to wait for three months at Whampoa, while the businessmen in the Canton 'factories' transacted the legitimate trade in tea. Each honest Jack Tar was allowed two visits to the Canton waterfront in parties of twenty. These were the occasions when the Chinese became familiar with the cultural and graceful way of life of the West. Mine hosts at intimate bars in Hog Lane, which ran for a distance of 200 yards between the Parsee and English warehouses, welcomed the eager visitors with shouts in pidgin, 'Halloo Jack! Fine day, old boy!' and with an encouraging cocktail, Canton Gunpowder, which comprised alcohol, tobacco juice, sugar and arsenic. When their escorting officers emerged from civil and reminiscent exchanges with friends in the factories, they usually set about quelling a race riot and assisting beaten-up and robbed sailors to the waiting lighters.   Seasoned travellers took the precaution on filling bladders and teapots with grog to bear aboard their ships, where liquor, very properly, was forbidden.   The bladders could be lowered or forced down a sailor's trousers and a carefully nursed teapot testified to the bearer's temperance.

It must be confessed that social behaviour on these tourist days at Canton lent sanction to the public notices which the Chinese authorities posted up in advance as warning of a guided tour.   The language is as xenophobic as today's pronouncements on international matters by China's Foreign Minister, but the difference in rhetorical style between the Hoppo's rounded periods and the Communist invective is the difference between an Oriental Gibbon and a shrill street-arab.

'About this time the devil ships are arriving and it is feared that lawless vagabonds will again tread their old habits,' a public announcement by the Hoppo reads. 'It is highly important that all have regard for their face and repent bitterly of their previous faults.   Let them not dare to employ young boys as servants to lead them to brothels nor to bring prostitutes into the Factories. . . It is the duty of the Hong merchants continually to instruct the Barbarians.   Since our Hong merchants are men of property and good family, it becomes them to have a tender regard for their face, not to cheat but to trade justly and so win devil confidence.'

It was an unnatural world, in which East and West met on common grounds of pretence and expedience, corruption and logic, hypocrisy and morality.   Neither really understood the other, but both had cooperated in building a system which each understood and from which each benefitted.   Each had contempt for the other, but the East showed it and the West tried to conceal it. The Westerners had a grudging respect for the top Chinese, which the Chinese seldom reciprocated; this was perhaps one explanation for the ultimate Chinese defeat.

'Study the past,' as Confucius — no Hoppo he — once said, 'if you would divine the future'.

THE ANTAGONISTS

William Jardine and James Matheson were the most successful opium runners and accordingly the most successful traders on the China coast. They were both Scottish, both religious in the stiff Calvinist way, both scrupulous in financial and personal matters, both indifferent to moralistic reflections on contraband and drugs. They even bear a superficial facial resemblance in their earlier portrait studies by George Chinnery, the talented and eccentric Irish painter who had holed up in Macao, fleeing from an ugly wife and uglier debts in Calcutta.

Jardine was the older and tougher, and the planner; everyone recalls that he kept no chair save his own in his office — visitors never sat down. Matheson was the organisation man, the administrator; he had the only piano in Macao, but no one laughed when he sat down to play.

Matheson could write a dry criticism of a ship-master in the company's employ: 'The *Gazelle* was unnecessarily delayed at Hong Kong in consequence of Captain Crocker's repugnance to receiving opium on the Sabbath. We have every respect for persons entertaining strict religious principles, but we fear that very godly people are not suited for the drug trade. Perhaps it would be better that the Captain should resign'.

Jardine could write a letter to a Prussian missionary, who spoke Chinese, persuading him to ship aboard an opium clipper and use his linguistic talent to dispense illicit drugs as well as God's word: 'We have no hesitation in stating to you that our principal reliance is on opium. Though it is our earnest wish that you should not in any way hinder the grand object you have in view (i.e. distributing the Bible in Chinese and delivering sermons in Chinese to the heathen) by appearing interested in what by many is considered an immoral traffic; yet such traffic is so absolutely necessary to give any vessel a reasonable chance of defraying her expenses that we trust you will have no objection to interpret on every occasion when your services may be requested'.

The Prussian divine, the Rev. Charles Gutzlaff, a monstrous religious fraud, who had been combining pill and ointment peddling with his hell-fire evangelism, sought guidance in prayer and meditation and piously embraced the opium runners.

The British Government — Whig or Tory — condoned the opium trade but was ashamed of it. 'Opium is not a necessity of life but a pernicious article of luxury, which ought not to be permitted, except for purposes of foreign commerce only, and which the Government should carefully restrain from internal consumption,' said Warren Hastings, Governor-General of India, in 1735. Opium became a major export-earner for British India and a national habit in China. The amount of opium reaching China rose from 20,000 chests in the 1833-34 season to 30,000 in 1835-36 and was well over 40,000 in 1837 (worth, say, four million pounds), when the number of floating warehouses at Lintin had risen from five to twenty-five.

The Imperial Dragon, last of the Manchus, while gathering his share of the 'squeeze' in Peking, became aware that, overall, the foreign trade was beginning to bleed the nation of silver. His personal rake-off was being offset by customs losses. More silver was being paid out to buy illicit opium than was being collected from the sale of tea, silk and that rhubarb for which the foreign devils had such a puzzling predilection.

With admirable timing, there now appeared the doomed figure of an honest and incorruptible opium hater — Governor-General Lin Tse-hsu of Hu-Kuang (the Hunan and Kwang Tung Province), who had cleaned up opium smoking in his province and was serenely confident that he could clean it up in Canton and throughout China. His methods were simple enough: he demanded that all opium pipes and all supplies of opium be surrendered. After the lapse of his benevolent notice of warning, he beheaded or strangled publicly every one who was discovered to be in possession of opium or an opium pipe. He sacked corrupt police and officials. The response had been highly encouraging.

The Dragon studied Lin's Memorials, summoned him to the Forbidden Palace, discussed his plans and then sent him to Canton, with overriding powers as Viceroy and High Commissioner to end the opium trade and restore the flow of silver. It is related by Maurice Collis, in his classic *Foreign Mud,* that the Viceroy who was being replaced and who was up to his peacock collar in the opium 'squeeze', 'fell into a swoon which lasted an hour,' when he heard of Lin's appointment.

The supreme irony, which was yet to emerge, was that Lin's British opponent, the distinguished naval officer and Superintendent of Trade, Captain Elliot, was as strongly opposed to opium smuggling as High Commissioner Lin was himself. The embarrassed diplomatic course which Elliot was compelled to pursue — to the destruction of both Lin and himself — led tortuously but inevitably to the birth of Hong Kong.

Before the coming of Lin, there had been some alarums and excursions between Canton, Macao and Lintin, when a tragic minor figure, Lord Napier, appointed Superintendent of Trade at Canton by Palmerston, tried to demolish the regulations imprisoning the foreign devils in their factories, and to open China to free trade. (Palmerston had stressed the Government's equivocal attitude towards opium smuggling in his instructions to Napier:'It is not desirable that you should encourage such adventures. But you must never lose sight of the fact that you have no authority to interfere with them or prevent them.')

Napier was humiliated and fooled by the Chinese. After a halt in Macao, he proceeded to Canton to try to present a 'letter'

— not a 'petition', as the regulations demanded — to the Viceroy. The Chinese called Napier 'Barbarian Eye' meaning that he was a diplomat and not a trader and accordingly an illegal immigrant in Canton, and used two ideographs to give a Chinese equivalent to his name which meant 'Laboriously Vile'. The affable Hong merchants were ordered to get rid of him, and the port was closed to trade.

Napier, inflamed by Jardine, who was now recommending the use of force, urged His Majesty's Government to despatch a military expedition to extort a commercial treaty and to seize Hong Kong, which, because of its excellent harbour, would constitute a base for the British and render them independent of Macao. Napier had at last written Hong Kong into the earliest staff plans for the Opium War.

In the outcome, Napier recklessly summoned two frigates from Lintin. They forced the narrows of the Bogue, with Captain Elliot following, impassive in an unarmed cutter, protected by an umbrella and disdainful of the execrably aimed cannonballs from the Chinese batteries. The Viceroy simply blocked the approach to Canton past Whampoa with sunken barges and threatened similarly to cut off the frigates' retreat. So it was Napier, broken and dying, who eventually retreated from Canton with the face-saving explanation that 'he did not feel authorised at present by the continued maintenance of his claim to occasion the further interruption of the trade of the port.' The unhappy envoy died in Macao — where the convent bells were hushed to allow him to sleep—and was buried in the foreign-devil cemetery.

This reverse for the British unhappily strengthened the fatal conviction of the formidable new Viceroy, Lin, that the British barbarians offered no military threat to China. 'Their vessels are successful only on the outer seas; it is their speciality to break the waves and sail under great winds,' he reported to the Dragon Seat. 'Once in harbour they become unwieldly. . . Their soldiers do not know how to use fists and swords. Also their legs are firmly bound with cloth and in consequence it is very inconvenient for them to stretch. Therefore what is called their power can be controlled without difficulty.'

This very wise mandarin was underrating British military power just as the not very wise Napier had underrated Chinese diplomatic finesse. The recurrent pattern of mutual misunderstanding becomes painfully familiar.

'Of all the Chinamen I have ever seen,' wrote Frederick Wells Williams, an American missionary and eye-witness in Macao, 'Lin was decidedly the finest looking and the most intelligent. He was indeed a very superior man, and if he had only been better informed he might have brought the difficult business intrusted to him to a much more creditable issue than he did; but this his ignorance and the conceit that accompanies ignorance prevented . . . He was naturally much elated at his rank and the absolute power entrusted to him led him to commit acts of rashness which recoiled upon himself'.

ELLIOT'S RETREAT

The formidable Jardine-Matheson team was operating its old one-two tactics. Matheson went to England in 1835 and launched what can be seen now to have been the first public-relations job ever undertaken in Britain on behalf of war. Jardine stayed in Macao. Matheson organised British commercial and trading support: send the gunboats in! But the Iron Duke of Wellington, then posturing as Foreign Secretary, scrawled his immortal rejection of the papers: 'That which we require now is, not to lose the enjoyment of what we have got.' — 'A cold-blooded fellow,' Matheson reported bitterly to Jardine. 'A strenuous advocate for submissiveness and servility.'

Palmerston came back with the Whigs under Lord Melbourne, but Matheson could not move him either. Jardine was to have more success when he came to London on retirement in 1839, just before Lin took over, and Matheson returned

to Macao, seriously considering whether the 'Princely Hong'
(as Jardine and Matheson was now known) should not retreat
to Manila.

Lin, the corpulent, grey-bearded, black-moustached mandarin, full of new-broom assurance and Chinese superiority,
had struck immediately: 'Let the Barbarians deliver to me every
particle of opium on board their storeships.   There must not be
the slightest atom concealed or withheld.   And at the same time
let the said Barbarians enter into a bond never hereafter to bring
opium in their ships and to submit, should any be brought, to
the extreme penalty of the law.'   The Chinese Hong merchants
were also ordered to bring the foreign devils into line; otherwise
one or two of them would be strangled to encourage the rest.
The rattled foreign traders, impressed by the fears of the Hong
men who had become their friends, offered 1,000 chests, which
Lin furiously rejected, contending correctly enough that this
was only a negligible proportion of the stores on hand, let alone
in Lintin.   Two Hong merchants arrived, pitiful in chains, to
use the pressure of their impending fate.   Lin peremptorily
ordered Dent, an elderly British trader with experience second
only to Jardine and Matheson, to attend him.   The factories
were under siege.   The traders went twice to divine service that
Sunday in the church inside the British factory.

Then Captain Elliot, Old Faithful, respected but disliked
by the merchants who knew he disapproved of their smuggling,
arrived breathless, hoisted the Union Jack above the British
factory, noted the strength of the enveloping Chinese naval
and military forces, sold out (as the merchants said), handed
over to Lin 20,000 chests of opium (worth at least two million
pounds), and on his own recognizance promised the British
owners full compensation by the Government.   Viceroy Lin
wrote to Elliot: 'The real sincerity and faithfulness shown are
worthy of praise.'

Lin went further; in his sober exultation, he even wrote to
the youthful Queen Victoria: 'We have reflected that this noxious

article is the clandestine manufacture of artful schemers under the dominion of your honourable nation. Doubtless you, the honourable chieftainness, have not commanded the growing and sale thereof. . . We have heard that in your honourable barbarian country the people are not permitted to inhale the drug. If it is admittedly so deleterious, how can your seeking profit by exposing others to its malefic power be reconciled with the decrees of Heaven?

'You should immediately have the plant plucked up by the very roots. Cause the land then to be holed up afresh, sow the five grains, and, if any man dare again to plant a single poppy, visit his crime with condign punishment. Then not only will the people of the Celestial Kingdom be delivered from an intolerable evil, but your own barbarian subjects, albeit forbidden to indulge, will be safeguarded against falling a prey to temptation. There will result for each the enjoyment of felicity. . . .

'On receipt of this letter, let your reply be speedy, advertising us of the measures you propose to adopt. Do not by false embellishments evade or procrastinate. Earnestly reflect hereon. Earnestly obey. And then displaying a devout sense of duty and a clear apprehension of celestial principles, you will have the approbation of the great sages and Heaven will ward away from you all calamities.'

One is impelled again to contrast these rolling periods with the dull bluster and repetitive invective of today's Communist mandarins. Their arrogance is the same. But Marxist dialectic blunts all wit and sours all style. Unfortunately it appears that Queen Victoria did not receive this admonition; her reactions would have been interesting. But Palmerston must have seen it; he was urbane but he could be choleric.

Many of Victoria's subjects would of course have agreed with Lin's strictures on the opium trade. Indeed in the Commons debate on the war, as we shall see, Gladstone, then a rising Tory star of only thirty years, took precisely the same line.

Captain Elliot, the moralist, would also have agreed. But Captain Elliot, the gallant if harassed naval commander, was now set on a collision course even if, paradoxically, it bore temporarily the appearance of retreat. After surrendering the opium, he jibbed at Lin's next order that all British traders must sign personal bonds of life and death before bringing their ships again to Whampoa. He abandoned Canton and fell back on Macao, where the Portuguese greeted the British with less than their customary warmth. Some ships were also sent to Hong Kong, to anchor in the roads between the great bare rock of the island and the straggling huts of Kowloon. The Americans, neutral and submissive, remained in Canton and prospered: they later handled trade for the absent British by proxy, and they also sold some ships to Lin for use against the British.

Lin let the British go; their cupidity, he was sure, would bring them back to Canton. He would use pressure to get them out of Macao; the Portuguese were always neutral — and amenable. The thought of British reinforcement and counter-measures did not seem to cross his mind.

How long Lin would have allowed the British to remain ashore in Macao and at anchor in Hong Kong can only be conjectured. He intended to have them back in Canton on his terms in time to resume normal trade. He had pledged the Dragon that he would do this. He had three months before September, the normal opening of the trading season. He privately warned the Portuguese Governor (His Excellency Adriao Accacio da Silva Pinto) that the British were birds that sought to occupy the nests of others. H.E. brooded, and rolled his liquid eyes nervously when Elliot suggested privately that the British might collaborate with the Portuguese in the defence of Macao. Macao, alas, must preserve its honourable and traditional role of neutrality, he replied.

But Lin's tentative timetable was disrupted by another of those cultural encounters between East and West. At Kowloon, following an intensive tasting of a new vintage Canton Gunpowder, there was a mob fight in which visiting American wine-lovers as well as British sailors and Chinese fishermen were involved, and a Chinese was killed. Elliot refused to hand over a British seaman — no one had any idea who the killer had been — to Lin for strangling. Elliot punished several seamen and paid compensation to the dead man's family. That was as far he would — or could — go.

So Lin ordered all Chinese servants to quit British homes in Macao, requested Silva Pinto to deprive the British residents of food and water, and strengthened his military build-up outside Macao's boundary gate. Elliot perforce evacuated all the British, men, women and children, in a fleet of small vessels. At a day's notice they abandoned homes and belongings, and found themselves bound for an uncertain existence of indefinite duration aboard sixty or so crowded merchant vessels at anchor off a strange island called Hong Kong.

The Portuguese governor sorrowfully farewelled the exodus, bowed to the ladies and even handed some aboard. A week later he welcomed Lin and a military detachment to Macao for a triumphant circuit of the settlement. The Portuguese cannon roared a salute for Lin, recalling the similar consideration when the convent bells had been hushed for Milord Napier. This was the price of correct neutrality.

War was now inevitable, although Lin seriously believed that, having forced the British out of Macao, he would somehow force them back into Canton. But by inflicting hardship on tender British women and innocent British children, driving them from their homes, threatening them with death or worse, and humiliating the British flag — as the exodus was naturally represented — Lin had given Palmerston a counter to the awkward argument that war would be primarily concerned with the defence of opium smuggling.

Again Lin tightened the screw — after a whiff of grapeshot off Kowloon, between three RN cutters and three Chinese junks which had refused to sell supplies to the British merchant fleet. Technically this shooting, which drove the junks ashore, marked the opening of the war: September 5, 1839. Lin announced that he would destroy the merchant fleet by cannon from Kowloon and fire-ships unless it was brought from Hong Kong into the Pearl estuary.

Elliot now had two frigates and he decided to fight. Outside Chuenpee Point, where forts protected the entrance to the Bogue, the two frigates, *Volage* and *Hyacinth,* ran up the long Chinese line of 29 anchored men-of-war, gave them their starboard broadsides at a distance of only fifty yards, turned and let them have the larboard broadside on the return tack. The Chinese cannon were sighted for a longer range and damaged only the frigates' rigging and wounded one seaman. In 45 minutes, four of the men-of-war had been sunk and the remainder so damaged that they could not have struggled up the Bogue if Elliot, never bloody-minded, had not called off the action.

Lin, in Chinese naval tradition, reported a Chinese victory, and the Emperor decorated him and the admiral.

THE GREAT OPIUM DEBATE

But this is not a combat history. Indeed, the Anglo-Chinese war was largely one of words. It is time to turn from China and look at the London home front — four months away in communications — where similar ignorance, confusion, intrigue and deception were bedevilling the British side.

Viscount Palmerston had been Foreign Secretary for nine years save for a brief break when the Tories came back. He overshadowed Lord Melbourne, the Prime Minister, and was no Little Englander, as Afghanistan could testify. He first saw Jardine in September 1839, at a time when Matheson's earlier evangelic work among the Manchester and London trading faithful was beginning to bear fruit. Petitions for enforced resumption of normal trade with the Chinese heathen, for payment of the two million pounds in compensation for the surrendered opium, and for reimbursement for the loss of textiles left behind in the Canton factories were piling up.

Jardine sold his argument for punitive action and martial promotion of British interests and free trade as effectively as he sold opium and goods. He did so in the face of many delicate political and humanitarian objections. There was strong popular opposition to the opium traffic among influential people in Britain — as there had been to the slave traffic, which the Whigs, and not the Tories, had abolished. The Whig governmental record was far more liberal than the Tory record. But Jardine had facts and figures, authority and local knowledge. He had his own maps and his astonishing 'paper of hints' — which was nothing less than a documented directive for military action in the Far East, outlining proposed policy, and even suggesting the number of troops that would be required. This Jardine 'paper' became the staff plans for the war that could no longer be deferred. Jardine would have made his mark as admirably as a soldier as he did as a *taipan* ('Great Manager'). Palmerston accepted his advice and by December the Cabinet had accepted Palmerston's. In February 1840, Palmerston quietly ordered the British authorities in India to send an expeditionary force to the China coast, to rendezvous on Jardine's suggestion in Hong Kong by June. Hong Kong, of course, was not yet a British colony, nor did anyone in the British Government dream at that time that it would become one. But it was already a British base.

Naturally the news leaked. An Opposition member inquired in early March about rumours of a sea battle between the Chinese and the Royal Navy at some place with the absurd name of Chuenpee. He was told, truthfully, that no official report had yet been received of the action. (It did not arrive until March 20 — nearly five months after the battle.) The Government then informed the Commons that certain preparations were being made to despatch an expedition from Calcutta, 'to obtain reparations for insults, an indemnification for wrongful losses of merchants' property, and security for future trade.' No Tory could reasonably object to these aspirations. Finally, the Tory leader, Sir Robert Peel, resolved to launch a censure motion against governmental mismanagement and ineptitude in the Far East, and in particular — as revealed, it was claimed, in ministerial papers — Palmerston's failure to instruct Captain Elliot promptly and adequately. Peel hoped that his side could soft-pedal the opium issue.

Some highlights from the debate, in which several distinguished figures participated, leave no doubt that obscurantism was not confined to the Forbidden City and the Dragon Seat.

Thomas Babington Macaulay, 39-year-old Secretary for War, was in fine fettle. He denounced Lin's barbarities, his menaces to British women with babes at breast, his Oriental insults to the British flag and Her Gracious Majesty.

'There is a limit to our forbearance,' he cried. 'I was much touched, and I believe others were also, by one passage contained in the despatch of Captain Elliot, in which he communicated his arrival at the factory in Canton. The moment at which he landed he was surrounded by his countrymen in an agony of despair at their situation, but the first step which he took was to order the flag of Great Britain to be taken from the boat and to be planted in the balcony. This was an act which revived the drooping hopes of those who looked to him for protection. It was natural that they should look with confidence on the victorious flag which was hoisted over them, which reminded them that they belonged to a country unaccustomed to defeat, to submission or to shame — it reminded them that they belonged to a country which had made the farthest ends of the earth ring with the fame of her exploits in redressing the wrongs of her children; that made the Bey of Algiers humble himself to her insulted consul; that revenged the horrors of the Black Hole on the fields of Plassey; that had not degenerated since her Great Protector vowed that he would make the name Englishman as respected as had ever been the name of Roman citizen.'

Mr Macaulay was perhaps less convincing when he discussed the opium trade. How could Captain Elliot be instructed to bring this traffic under control? It would have been beyond his power to execute any such order, no matter with what authority he had been invested. Smuggling into England could not be stopped with a large, efficient and expensive preventive service. How immense a staff would Captain Elliot need to suppress smuggling into China?

The Secretary for War then told the House officially for the first time that Britain was going to war with China: 'I beg to declare my earnest desire that this most rightful quarrel may be prosecuted to a triumphal close, that the brave men to whom is entrusted the task of demanding that reparation which the circumstances of the case require, may fulfil their duties with moderation, but with success, that the name not only of English valour, but of English mercy, may be established.'

Despite the strong reservations of his leader and party, William Ewart Gladstone, an independent and idealistic 30, soon dropped any pretence of speaking to the motion and launched into a scathing attack on the opium trade. Ironically, both Lin and Elliot would have applauded his diatribe, and Lin, in lofty mandarin, might have matched his eloquence.

'I will ask the noble Lord a question. Does he know that the opium smuggled into China comes exclusively from British ports, that is from Bengal and through Bombay? We require no preventive service to put down this illegal traffic. We have only to stop the sailings of the smuggling vessels; it is a matter of certainty that if we stopped the exportation of opium from Bengal, and broke up the depot at Lintin, and checked the cultivation of it in Malwa, and put a moral stigma on it, we should greatly cripple, if not extinguish, the trade in it.

'The great principles of justice are involved in this matter. You will be called upon, even if you escape from condemnation on this motion, to show cause for your present intention of making war upon the Chinese. They gave us notice to abandon the contraband trade. When they found that we would not, they had the right to drive us from their coasts on account of our obstinacy in persisting in this infamous and atrocious traffic. I am not competent to judge how long this war may last, but this I can say, that a war more calculated in its progress to cover this country with permanent disgrace, I do not know and have not read of.'

Most of the other speeches were dull and rambling, but Palmerston, in rebuttal, was in his best debating form, masterful and facetious. On the central issue of the inadequacy of his instructions to Captain Elliot: 'I have been blamed because they were not long enough. Gentlemen who make long speeches think, I suppose, that I should write long letters. They imagine that precise instructions contained in a few but significant words are not proportioned to the length that they have to travel; they imagine that when you write to China your letter should be as long as the journey.'

He stressed that the Opposition — with the exception of Gladstone — had not urged in the motion that any measures should be taken to curtail poppy-growing in Bengal; in any event, would there then not ensue uncontrolled cultivation in Turkey, Persia or Indian states in whose internal administration Britain had no say? He believed that the Emperor of China was a very different person from his Commissioner Lin, and would be eager to end the dispute quickly and amicably. Palmerston then read a petition from the China trade firms, organised by Jardine and Matheson, which insisted that, 'unless measures of the Government are followed up with firmness and energy, the trade with China can no longer be conducted with security to life and property, or with credit or advantage to the British nation.'

That was a good strong Tory argument on which to close. Even so, it was, as the old Iron Duke would have said, a damned close-run thing: the Government defeated the censure by only nine votes.

HONG KONG: THE UGLY DUCKLING CHANGELING

The British expedition — 16 men-of-war and 31 vessels, carrying 4,000 Irish, Scotch and Indian troops — arrived in Hong Kong waters in June 1840. The Commander-in-Chief was Rear Admiral George Elliot, a cousin of Captain Elliot, a coincidental appointment which must have persuaded many Chinese that family nepotism was not confined to the Middle Kingdom. The expedition, incidentally, was larger than Jardine's recommendation in his 'paper of hints' — a tribute both to his Scottish sense of economy and his greater knowledge, because it soon became evident that a smaller force could have prevailed.

Lin was as confident and resolute, as misinformed and as deluded, as ever. He strengthened fortifications, issued pronouncements and placed prizes on captured Englishmen and their vessels and weapons ($25,000 for a 74-gun man-of-war, and $5,000 for Elliot's head), adding such nice touches as: 'Court officials will not be permitted to deduct their customary ten percent "squeeze", and captured white seamen or foot soldiers will be worth $100 a head, compared with only $20 for their coloured counterparts.'

The ludicrous 'war' lurched forward in two instalments. The British demands, as laid down by Jardine to Palmerston, were: apology for insult, payment of the costs of the expedition and also full repayment of the value of the 20,000 chests of opium, and a treaty for free trade with China at Canton, Amoy, Foochow, Ningpo and Shanghai, plus rejection of all Hong intermediaries and recognition of the rank of British consuls as equivalent to a mandarin.

The British ships moved up the China coast, tried vainly to serve their demands on the terrified Chinese at Amoy under a Western-style white flag of truce (which the Chinese thought must mean that there were dead aboard, probably cholera victims, as white is the Chinese funeral colour). They finally seized Ting-hai on the Chusan Islands, at the entrance to the Yangtze, without opposition, and boldly entered the Pei-ho, approach to Peking. The astounded Emperor was confronted, amazingly, with Western cannon. The foreign devil, literally, was at the gate.

The Dragon manifested the same scruples, fairness, logic and deception that had marked the behaviour of both sides from the outset. He ordered Lin, blandly stiffening morale in by-passed Canton, to be put in chains: 'You have dissembled to Us, disguising in your despatches the true colour of affairs. So far from having been of any help, you have caused the waves of confusion to arise. A thousand interminable disorders are sprouting. You have behaved as if your arms were tied. You are not better than a wooden image. And as We contemplate your grievous failings, We fall a prey to anger and melancholy. Your official seals shall immediately be taken from you and, with the speed of flames, you shall hasten to Peking, where We will see how you may answer Our questions. Respect this! Tremble intensely and obey! The words of the Emperor!'

The Emperor gave the Manchu mandarin, Kishen, the task of deceiving the foreign devils in the Pei-ho by persuading them to return to Canton, where he would of course pretend to accept their demands while assembling his troops: 'After prolonged negotiation has made the Barbarians weary and exhausted, We can suddenly attack them and thereby subdue them.'

Kishen was clearly a smooth dog in the smoothest traditions of the Summer Palace. He was perhaps the wealthiest mandarin in China. He had none of the honest dedicated scruples of the miserable Lin. He flattered the honest Elliot seadogs. He 'conned' them into going back to Canton: 'I can assure you that His Majesty is most graciously inclined. He understands how provoking Lin must have been, and loving, as he does, strangers from afar, you may rest assured of his best condescension. Let us adjourn . . . to the provincial city and I can promise you that you will be wholly satisfied.'

It is a tragedy that Jardine was not there at that time. Back in England, he was getting ready to run for Parliament — but with only three more years to live. He would have ended this burlesque outside Peking, and would have saved China the final crushing humiliation of the second instalment of the Anglo-Chinese war. But the Elliots trustingly pulled out, and Kishen reported to the Dragon: 'Although the Barbarians are brave and defiant, and scarcely amenable to reason, nevertheless they soon become well-disposed on receiving words of praise. Indeed, I found that even in a boastful mood they could be moderated by pleasant phrases. But Your Majesty is daily confronted with innumerable problems. These trifles do not warrant a turn of the Holy Glance.'

The original Elliot was in command at Canton for the interrupted *charivari*. His cousin the Admiral — fortunately for his reputation — had been invalided home. Captain Elliot soon discovered that he was being given the honourable run-around. After six weeks of nonsense, he suddenly got tough, seized the Chinese forts at the entrance to the Bogue, after killing and wounding a thousand Chinese without a single death on the British side. He could have taken and sacked Canton, but he held his hand — as was always his wont — and Kishen came mincing to heel. Elliot settled for cession of Hong Kong as the new, independent and invulnerable centre of British trade, reopened trade with China and an indemnity of six million dollars by annual instalments over six years. Opium, of course, would be stored at Hong Kong without any suggestion of breach of law. Kishen, like Elliot, thought he had done well. He would soon get the six million dollars back by 'squeeze'. But, as we have seen, both men were broken by their masters. The Emperor repudiated the agreement. He was very stupid. A Sir Henry Pottinger — good sound colonial name — replaced Elliot, a Kiying replaced Kinshen, and the second instalment of the war began in August 1841. This time there was real fighting near Nanking, where brave Manchu troops were destroyed, and the Dragon submitted. In 1842 the five ports were opened up, the Chinese paid the six million dollars for the opium which Elliot had handed over and which Lin had scrupulously destroyed. This item was chastely described as 'indemnity for property surrendered as ransom for the lives of British subjects'.

And Hong Kong, the ugly duckling changeling, remained, despised and unwanted, on the British colonial doorstep.

POST-MORTEM

Two sobering reflections. First, when the British expedition arrived in Hong Kong in June 1840 to repair by force the twelve month-old break with Canton, the opium trade had already recovered. Matheson had replaced the firm's lost 6,000 chests and was buying directly at Singapore. The British tea trade had been restored at Canton by Occidental cooperation with the accommodating Americans. Many of the evicted British families had drifted back to their Macao homes, where they discovered that their Portuguese neighbours had carefully protected and cared for their belongings.

Second, Hong Kong became more profitable and more convenient than Lintin for the handling of opium. Naturally, Peel's Tories, when they formed a government in 1842, did nothing to stem the contraband which their young Master Gladstone had so violently denounced. The number of chests sold for export totalled 20,000 a year in 1839, 39,000 in 1845 and 52,000 in 1850 — by which time India's revenue from opium was more than one-fifth its total income.

Jardine died (aged 58), as a back-bencher in the Commons, comforted by Matheson's assurances that Hong Kong — and the 'Princely Hong' — would do very well. Palmerston wrote a tribute to his counsellor in 1842: 'It is extraordinary that the information which Mr Jardine so handsomely provided and which was embodied in the instructions which we issued in February 1840 was so accurate and complete that it appears that our successors have not found reason to make any alterations . . . There is no doubt that this event (the Nanking treaty), which will form an epoch in the progress of the civilisation of the human races, must be attended with the most important advantages to the commercial interests of England.' Elliot would not have endorsed that grandiloquent reference to 'the progress of civilisation'. Nor would Lin. Nor would Gladstone. A mixed, but honest, team, who probably would have had little else in common.

Matheson, following Jardine as usual, secured election to the same seat which Jardine vacated, and died amidst crocuses instead of poppies at a magnificent home at Lewes. He was 82.

Britain and China entered into an agreement in 1907 to end the opium traffic, on condition that the Chinese curtailed the widespread production of the drug which they had belatedly begun, and the British reduced by one-tenth each year the exports from India. The long-range agreement ended satisfactorily in 1917, but by 1921 Chinese *tuchuns* or warlords had revived the cultivation of poppies to pay their troops from an opium tax. The British were very angry with this 'flagrant breach of treaty obligations' and threatened to go to the League of Nations. But there was no Emperor to approach, and there was no place to send gunboats. Finally the Communists took over and abolished opium in 1949. The British had decreed opium smoking illegal in Hong Kong in 1946.

PAST AS PROLOGUE?

So the opium went, but Hong Kong remained, developed, declined and flourished. The colony with the bad name survived bad governors, well-meaning governors, typhoons, fire, slump, war and occupation. First tents, then shanties, then buildings arose to house the Chinese who began to arrive and who were described by one administrator as 'the scum of Canton'. Because they welcomed the security and comfort of prison, they used to be punished for their crimes by being flogged or having their pigtails cut off. 'You Can Go To Hong Kong For Me!' was a popular song of derogation in London in the 1850's. A book on China at that time had a chapter entitled: 'Hong Kong: Its Position, Prospects, Character and Utter Worthlessness from Every Point of View for England.'

Its early governors differed erratically on policy and gave little hope of today's close union between Government and Business. Sir Hercules Robinson tried to segregate Chinese and Westerners in order 'to protect the European and United States communities from the injury and inconvenience of intermixture with the Chinese'. Sir John Pope Hennessy (in the 1880's) went to the opposite extreme: he selected Chinese for government jobs and even wanted to give them the right to visit the public library. He was finally sent to Mauritius, where he was again fired for his desegregation heresies.

But slowly the colony found its hands and knees and then its feet—its entrepot trade, its shipping and its profits—chiefly because of the security and stability and opportunity assured by the Union Jack. At the beginning of the twentieth century, there were a quarter of a million Chinese in Hong Kong. The once bare rock progressed peacefully and profitably, and with a certain smugness, from the Victorian to the Edwardian period, pinning its faith in free trade, individualism and hard work. It ran into its first trouble with the China mainland in the twenties and thirties, when Chinese nationalism began to rise. In 1925 the disastrous boycott of British goods was organised by Chiang Kai-shek and, after six months, seemed likely to strangle the colony. Then came the Japanese: they took the New Territories and Kowloon in four days and the island in two weeks, in the colony's centenary year.

This, again, should have been Hong Kong's death-rattle, more particularly because Franklin Roosevelt said at the Atlantic Charter conference and again at Yalta that the colony should be internationalised or handed over to China. The place was in poverty and ruins when the Japanese withdrew, but Sir Robert Morse, the Governor of the Hongkong and Shanghai Bank, at a cost of seven million pounds, heroically redeemed all the unbacked currency which the Japanese had issued, and restored Hong Kong's credit, pride and prestige.

For a while the Chinese Nationalists — as anti-colonial, of course, as the Chinese Communists — made trouble in Hong Kong with propaganda, demonstrations and riots, on the same pattern in that recent yesterday as the Communists are initiating today. But Chinese labour and investment capital poured back: between 1946 and 1948 trade more than doubled; between 1948 and 1950 it doubled again. The Korean War embargo against China killed entrepot trade, but restless, resilient Hong Kong turned immediately and rewardingly to local industrial effort.

Because of the coincidence of the family name, I may perhaps be excused for recalling that a British Labour Member of Parliament named Emrys Hughes told Parliament in 1950 that Hong Kong could not be defended or supported and might profitably be bartered to the Communists for trade advantages. A columnist in the *South China Morning Post* wrote a spirited reply which, in the mock-facetious, serio-comic, enduring colonial mood of yesterday, still cockily reflects the irrational Hong Kong mood of today, and projects the illogical Hong Kong mood of tomorrow:

> *The vughes of Mr Emrys Hughes*
> *Provoke a wheen disgusted phughes!*
> *Wot, swap Hong Kong for I. O. Ughes?*
> *Out upon ugh, we refughes!*

Still, let us not be so obtughes
As to resent Hughes in the nughes.
Permit him rather to amughes,
Remember qui s'excughes s'accughes,
And he has naught to lughes.

Hong Kong Tomorrow

'I NEVER THINK OF THE FUTURE'

Since Chairman Mao set the shirt-tails of his Politburo chiefs
afire, and either uncovered or precipitated the great party rift
and struggle for power, it may well be doubted whether any one
in Peking has known what Chinese policy will, or should, be
in the next ten months, far less in the next ten years. To try,
therefore, to predict, or even speculate upon, Peking's long-
range intentions towards Hong Kong is to enter an unreal
world and to peddle dreams as prophesy.

In theory, Hong Kong and the New Territories remain
intact and inviolate until 1997, when the leased New Territories
revert to China. When that happens, Hong Kong's colonial
jugular will be cut, however tenaciously Britain has managed
to hang on to its sovereign rights over the island and Kowloon,
established by a Victorian-model 'unequal treaty'. On that
deadline, man will be on the moon, and it may fairly be presumed
that, atomic disaster or not, the Chinese people will have patiently
reshaped Maoist Communism as the Russians have reshaped
Leninist Communism over the past thirty years. It is surely as
unreasonable to think that Chairman Mao will still then be

alive as to think that the colonial status quo will have prevailed over the intervening period.

As in the past, Hong Kong's difficulties, emergencies and crises will continue to recur from year to year, either as single spies or in battalions. They will, one imagines, be resolved by showdown or compromise; but, with the tide of history and the flow of events continually running against the status quo, one thing is certain: the key to Hong Kong's future lies in Peking and not in Hong Kong.

The Hong Kong optimists, or ostriches, who think or pretend to think otherwise, are blind to the fate of Macao, Hong Kong's weak sister, and of Shanghai, Hong Kong's dark sister. The colonial role, style and mood of those two former strongholds of Western penetration into China differ markedly of course, from the Hong Kong phenomenon. But, as we shall see, there are lessons and portents in the circumstances of their decline and fall which, properly studied and accepted, could perhaps postpone or delay the inevitable in Hong Kong.

Maybe it is unfair to criticise the surface indifference of Hong Kong to change and the rewards of change. The Hong Kong mood, as we have seen, is one of masterly expedience and crisis-to-crisis adjustment and recovery. It is partly a gambler's mentality, partly fatalism. As in Shanghai, no foreigner came to Hong Kong to make a home there; he came to make a living and get out. Nor does any Chinese live in Hong Kong against his will. Foreign devils and Chinese alike can be said to be abiding by rules which are none the less binding because they have never been properly written. Even if these rules were backed by the same absolutism which prevailed a century ago, Peking could break them today whenever the colonial status quo lost its sanction of mutual reward.

It is virtually impossible to persude Hong Kong's Government or Establishment to discuss the future. Hong Kong is the city of the present — the City of the Five-Year-Return-of-Capital. Some hint that Five-Year-Return is being 'escalated' to Three-Year-Return. And why not? When you can't look ahead, why try?

In the Hong Kong Club, or the comfortable box of the Chief Steward of the Jockey Club at Happy Valley racecourse (next to the cemetery), they could well put up Einstein's crack: 'I never think of the future. It comes soon enough.' Or, better still, the apophthegm of Quintilian (which sounds today like something out of Chairman Mao): *'Praesente fortuna pejor est futuri'* — 'He is only anxious about the future to whom the present is unprofitable.'

Hong Kong's predicament and prospects acquire proper perspective when examined against the backdrop of Shanghai and Macao — and, to a lesser degree, Singapore. If Macao is Hong Kong's weak sister, and Shanghai is Hong Kong's dark sister, Singapore is Hong Kong's half-sister. The operative word in Singapore, explicitly, is *Chinese* — just as, by implication, it always was in Macao and Shanghai, and still is in Hong Kong.

DARK SISTER, DEAD

Hong Kong was born of 'foreign mud' (the Chinese term for opium). Shanghai was born in Chinese mud — the muddy shore of the Whangpoo River, on which the British intruders, their visas granted by Jardine, Matheson and Palmerston and validated by gunpowder, first landed in 1843 (Year of the Hare, which sometimes devours its young). There they stickily floundered, cleaned the mud off their boots, and remained, free-wheeling and fortune-making, for over a century. With the unwelcome but unavoidable aid of rival adventurers from a dozen other foreign countries, they laid the foundations of China's largest, wickedest, most exciting city on that Whangpoo mud, which became the richest real estate in the Far East. The good earth of China and the good mud of Shanghai were one and the same.

The foreign devils built the International Settlement and Frenchtown. They swallowed more than a score of neighbouring Chinese villages. They imposed their own foreign laws and regulations. They enforced extra-territoriality (or extrality, to use the simpler Shanghai term). They survived war and revolution, strikes and bombs, booms and depressions. They were refloated by incredible strokes of luck at times when their fortunes seemed to have fatally ebbed. Their modern, Western-style skyscrapers climbed higher and higher as their appalling Chinese-style slums spread wider and wider.

They never really got that Whangpoo mud out of their fingernails. They never learned — except how to make more money. They never adjusted. At least, they were not as surprised when the Communists took over in 1949 as they had been when Chiang Kai-shek's new planes, by Freudian error, bombed the International Settlement instead of Japanese war-ships in 1937.

It was not that they had power without responsibility, but that they had power without ever thinking of responsibility — which, I guess, is the difference between the prerogative of a whore and the prerogative of a pianist in a whorehouse.

This, we shall see, is one of the several decisive differences between Hong Kong and Shanghai. They were sisters under their mud; they were both in a sense the colonel's lady; but Hong Kong has learned and survived, and Shanghai never learned and so died: the dark victim, ironically, of a system which envisaged attack only from outside, and not, as it transpired, from within.

It is impossible to speculate upon Hong Kong's future without considering Shanghai's past.

Shanghai, as a Communist party official told me gloomily when I returned after an absence of sixteen years, was 'untamed'. It is still 'untamed', another decade later. This is no light charge. 'Untamed' has always been a grave Chinese accusation, whether applied to the deviations of the Yellow River ('China's Sorrow') or the deviations of a 'rightist's' heart (Mao's Sorrow).

Shanghai (meaning 'above the sea') was a squalid, fourth-rate, walled city of 100,000 people when the British gunboat blasted the Woosung forts with her 32-pounders and opened the mud-flats to opium, bibles and free trade. (The gunboat, first steamship ever to double the Cape of Good Hope, was, by macabre chance, named *Nemesis*.) The commander, who had been intrigued by the style of the Son of Heaven's pronouncements from the Forbidden City, spent some time compiling a scholarly declaration which amused the crew of *Nemesis* but which must have raised eyebrows in the Admiralty: 'Under the canopy of Heaven and within the circumference of the Earth, many are the different countries. Of the multitude of these, no one is there that is not ruled by the Supreme Heavenly Father, nor are there any that are no brethren of one family. Being then of one family, very plain is it that they should hold friendly and brotherly intercourse together, and not boast themselves one above the other.' Jolly good show.

Shanghai persisted and flourished because it could levy tribute on all the wealth, trade and lifeblood of the Yangtze valley, with half the total population and half the total trade of all China. Its location was immeasurably superior to Hong Kong's. The foreign devils persisted and flourished — 60,000 in a city (in the thirties) of four million Chinese — because they ran the show, controlled government, finance, customs revenue, and, in two-thirds of the area, were not subject to Chinese courts or law (good old 'extrality'). Under their autocracy, Shanghai grew up chained, if not really tamed. The new industrial and commercial China was controlled by the Western-bossed twelve square miles of the International Settlement and the French Concession.

Shanghai was far more than a glittering, if doomed, monument to ruthless Western imperialism. The Chinese Communist Party was born in Shanghai, four decades ago. Chinese industry, Chinese capitalism and the Chinese trade union movement were all spawned in Shanghai. The metropolis became a sanctuary for defeated warlords, international criminals, political exiles, rival tong bosses and White Russian exiles. Chou En-lai was only one of the many Communist leaders who, from time to time, as their political fortunes seesawed, quietly took up residence in the high-walled villas and hidden gardens of tree-lined Frenchtown, plotting the downfall of all that Shanghai and the thirteen flags of its barbarian masters represented.

Mao Tse-tung, in his youth, once went to Shanghai for one of the provisional meetings of the embryonic party, but could not find the address. Mao has never liked or trusted Shanghai. Chou En-lai — like Ho Chi-minh — also sought refuge in Hong Kong, but neither ever plotted its downfall. Perhaps each recognised that it had inbuilt advantages for China which Shanghai never pretended to have. Also only one colonial flag flew in Hong Kong; the thirteen rival flags in Shanghai must have held brighter promise of disunity and distrust.

Shanghai was also the headquarters of the powerful secret society called the 'Greens', whose Chinese bosses ran the underworld and the police in Frenchtown.

Finally, Shanghai was a bloody centre in the opening of the long, brutal Japanese war against China — in 1937, only six years before the centenary of the British seizure of the City of the Mud-Flats. Japanese marines fought Chinese regulars in the narrow alleys and open fields and across the canals of Outer Shanghai, while an international force of US marines, British soldiers and the Shanghai Volunteer Corps stood uneasily on guard behind the flimsy sandbag and barbed wire barricades which protected the approaches to Frenchtown, the International Settlement and the holy Bund.

There was at that time no actual fighting inside the Settlement. But this 1937 fighting of Asians against Asians marked the real and historical end of the Shanghai that the West had built, just as the triumphant 1949 march of the disciplined Red armies into Shanghai marked the real and historical imposition of Communist rule over China. (When Shanghai fell, so also did Chiang Kai-shek's last hopes.) If they had not been Communist troops, they would have been Nationalist troops. The only thing that mattered was that they were Chinese troops. An exultant Chinese population greeted their compatriot saviours.

The essential and continuing difference between Shanghai yesterday and Hong Kong today — and tomorrow (for how long?) — is that the great mass of Chinese in Hong Kong want no deliverance by Communist troops.

Hong Kong is China, but it is not yet Communist China. Of course, the foreign devils are not really loved by Hong Kong's poor or wealthy Chinese, but they are not hated, as the Shanghai foreign devils were hated. Hong Kong has avoided the excesses of Shanghai's suicidal autocracy. Obviously Hong Kong will need to be even more adroit and alert in the future, but on past evidence the necessary realism should not be lacking. The foreign devil known to the Hong Kong Chinese adult is still better than the Communist devil, whom he also knows and whom the younger Chinese generation in Hong Kong suspects if it doesn't really know.

There were fatal flaws in the Shanghai design. There was a doomed recklessness. *Laisser-faire* became anarchy. The Shanghai Municipal Council overrode the foreign consuls. Instructively and appropriately, the foundations of the International Settlement, and a united foreign-devil front, were laid when the Americans asked to be allowed to put their extra-territorial prisoners in the British jail.

Shanghai was identified with the sack of the Summer Palace in Peking. Shanghai was a dead loss to Peking and the rest of China. Hong Kong is still a clear gain. The richer Shanghai became, the poorer the ineffective Chinese government became, — as, for example, during the boom in silver, when silver resources, against futile Peking protests, were exported.

Shanghai was a self-appointed, self-ruling foreign state, not a British colony like Hong Kong. The maintenance of law and order in Shanghai rested in part on an understanding with the underworld. The interests of the Shanghai *taipan*, however piously dissembled, were inimical to the interests of China: they had to be for the system to work. The Chinese residents of the Settlement paid heavier municipal taxes than the foreign devils did. The 'Government' in Nanking abolished 'extrality' but Shanghai took no notice. Sir Victor Sassoon left India to avoid taxes and came to Shanghai to invest—but he knew enough to incorporate his companies in safer Hong Kong.

Thirteen different national flags were far too many. The elaborate Shanghai system had been massive enough to delay the inevitable takeover because as a rule those flags, in self-defence, flew together. But when the Japanese in Shanghai tried to go it alone, in sabotage of the *taipans'* unwritten law, they opened the system to destruction from within. And at that moment of truth — and betrayal — all the conditions for revolt in Shanghai were ripe, ready and waiting.

The May 1967 riots in Hong Kong showed that these conditions do not exist in the colony — yet.

*   *   *

When you approach Shanghai by ship today, the sea runs as choppily, as yellow and mud-stained as ever, and that strange haunting burnt-sweet smell, uniquely evocative of Shanghai, blows as headily as ever from the green mainland. Sampans and junks, with patched batwing sails and staring painted eyes on their prows, drift and dip past, fluttering the five-starred red flag of Mao, the Great Helmsman. The sinister blackened hulks of the opium barges are gone from their old moorings, and in the screened naval dockyards opposite, you are told, Polaris submarines are being assembled. Gone from the Bund and its Western skyline is the vast moored fleet of junks, which were once the mud-embalmed, clothing-festooned homes of tens of thousands of fishing, river and nomad families, who subsisted largely on what they could dredge from the dark waters of the Whangpoo.

*   *   *

Let me recall my first nostalgic return to Shanghai by ship ten
long years ago, and sixteen longer years after my original life
there.   During those sixteen years the Japanese had ruled Shanghai, the Americans had liberated it, Chiang Kai-shek had fled
from it, and Chairman Mao had absorbed it — only today to
be still struggling for it.

Meanwhile, Hong Kong had peacefully recovered from
Japanese occupation, had flourished, and had continued against
all the odds to prosper.

Despite the passage of time, and because of the current
'cultural' turmoil in Shanghai, I think that there is more than
anecdotal interest in my first glimpse of Communist Shanghai
— impressions which were strengthened by later visits.

I went to the Sunya restaurant on Nanking Road, my
favourite eating-house in the old days, and dined on luscious
prawns, birds-nest soup and tender beef with oyster sauce.
The English name had been removed from the door, but I had
not forgotten the number — 719.   The two floors were crowded,
as they always had been.   There was, I thought, little change
inside the restaurant — except the party exhortations in dramatic
white lettering on crimson banners.   The polished spittoons
were still beside the tables.   The waiters were still wearing
their rakish white yachting caps and white, slit-skirt gowns.
The diners — mostly family groups — were still eating noisily,
gaily, comfortably, abundantly.   The same stout barman — it
seemed to me — was pouring the same lively Tsingtao draught
beer into the same glass mugs with the same hearty disdain for
hygiene in his salvage of the swill in the tray.   And there was
the same rich enduring fragrance of good Chinese cooking.

'The food is the same,' my urbane waiter assured me in
excellent English, after accepting my explanation of my sixteen-
year absence.   'It is just as good.   The profit, maybe, goes
somewhere else.   It doesn't come to me, although they tell us
we are all going to share it some time.'   He grinned and jerked

his thumb upwards. 'But we are okay.' He eyed me sharply when, rejecting more beer, I asked for a whisky, brought me a half-empty bottle of White Horse, and with difficulty prised open its long-sealed and semi-embalmed stopper.

'This will cost you more than the dinner,' he warned me, filling the old familiar silver eggcup. 'We don't get any more whisky now. The price is fixed — ' For one awful moment, embarrassing to us both, I felt that he almost used the old forbidden honorific, 'master'.

He was right. The dinner, which was perfect, cost maybe eight shillings; the two straight whiskies cost more than sixteen shillings. Just before I left, he looked swiftly around, then, interposing his body between my cubicle and the cashier, poured me a third whisky — on the honourable house. We smiled together. No good party bet he. I still doubt if many Shanghai Chinese are. They had, gladly and justifiably, rejected the foreign devils. But they don't have to accept the foreign ideological delirium, nor the new tyranny from a Peking which every good Shanghai-born Chinese knows is provincial and still pigtailed. Nor, on all the evidence, are they doing so now.

There followed another incident on that same night, which, in retrospect, has an historic poignancy because it recalls the lost love between China and Russia, and an abiding interest because it stresses the absence of communication between the Chinese and the foreign devils. I went down Nanking Road to the Bund, where a Soviet cruiser and two destroyers, hung with white electric necklaces and giant red stars, were moored on a goodwill visit. I passed incautiously, wearing white open-neck shirt and slacks, under a green, crimson and purple pagoda spanning the road between the old Cathay and Palace hotels and was immediately engulfed by an hysterical, tightly packed crowd. In all those happily milling tens of thousands, there was not a single foreigner in sight save myself. To my consternation, I was at once mistaken for a Soviet naval officer.

There were welcoming shouts of '*So-lean!*' — an ironic phonetic confusion in view of my weight; it is the Chinese word for 'Russia'. I became the terrified, weakly smiling centre of a maelstrom of cheering, shouting, back-thumping, hand-shaking Chinese, intent on carrying me bodily aboard the Soviet cruiser. Most of them seemed to have dined heavily on garlic and stale fish. Members of the Communist Young Pioneers Corps tore off their red cravats and thrust them into my trembling hands. I made a mistake in passing over two grubby handkerchiefs in agitated exchange. This intensified the struggling, the shouts of '*So-lean!*' and the deep-throated chanting of the *Internationale*.

Four boys, two girls and an elderly man, carrying a baby on his back, came down heavily in the commotion. I managed to stand over two of the fallen until they scrambled up. Some men began to punch one another. Other excited Chinese thrust Communist enamel badges at me. I hastily produced a cheap ballpoint pen, two gnawed pencil butts and a half-empty matchbox from a Kobe night-club in guilty reciprocity. All I had left were my passport and wallet.

The guards aboard the Soviet cruiser were taking a keen interest in my approach, half-carried and half-dragged, towards the vessel's gangway. A red-faced, corpulent Russian officer in white uniform — who, I realised even in my agitation, looked remarkably like myself — bawled warnings at me through a megaphone.

Then a dozen white-helmeted, white-coated policemen charged in, drove back the cheering crowd, escorted me to an office and showed me through a side-door to a pedicab. I thanked them in what they perhaps imagined to be fluent Russian. They saluted and one nodded appreciatively at the red cravats which I was still clutching. I fear that they may have believed that I had been distributing red neckties on behalf of the Soviet.

At the dockside, two Chinese watchmen sternly checked the fare I paid the pedicab-driver, and thrust me back and struck him with a baton when I, forgetting the new order, tried to tip him.

*   *   *

Chairman Mao himself dislikes and distrusts Shanghai — and is probably more than a little scared of it. The Chinese leader who knows it best is discredited President Liu Shao-chi, who organised the Shanghai proletariat in those hard, early, dangerous days when, it is now alleged, he was cunningly plotting *against* Chairman Mao and the cause.

Today Shanghai allegedly has a population of more than ten million and is ringed with new satellite industrial towns. It is too big. And it is still growing. As the nation's oldest and greatest industrial centre, it has too large a population of the proletariat, whom Mao has never known, understood or trusted as he does his peasants. Then the Shanghai Chinese, like most big city dwellers, feels scorn for the rustic provincials in the rest of China, including Peking. He knows that Shanghai initiative, Shanghai shrewdness and Shanghai know-how is infinitely superior to Chinese talent elsewhere. He is more sophisticated, more sceptical, more adventurous, more informed, more independent, more individualistic — and more receptive, because of the city's Westernised background, to Western ideas.

As the Peking Maoists uneasily argue, he is heir to an amoral alien tradition; he has been tainted by foreign influence and habits; he must instinctively be motivated by unfraternal greed and self-interest.

So at the onset of 'liberation', the Communist party decided at first, not merely to 'tame' Shanghai, but to let it wither on the vine. (A deeper and darker problem would obviously arise if Hong Kong were 'liberated'.) In the fifties, Shanghai factories were being dismantled, a large-scale migration of skilled workers was organised, and imported raw materials were wastefully transported to remote inland factories.

For a time, whatever its hectic and turbulent past, Shanghai looked like a city without a future. But realism finally triumphed, and Shanghai was grudgingly accepted as an industrial centre which foreign devils had built on honest Chinese mud, but which the broad revolutionary masses might be able to use to advantage.

Shanghai's transformation is a useful guide to the likely fate of Hong Kong if the Communists took over the colony. There have been ambitious re-housing schemes, but the speed with which the red-tiled roofs of compact modern units are thrusting up amid the old grey tiles of Shanghai's slum areas lags behind the Hong Kong capitalist effort if estimated in relation to population. Industrial production in Hong Kong, on the same basis, is estimated to be ahead of the Shanghai record in the ratio 70:30. Shipping tonnage handled in Shanghai is still a deep, dark mystery, but certainly there can be no comparison with the maritime business of Hong Kong — 6,775 ocean-going ships in 1966, and more than 22 million tons of cargo, cleared more quickly than anywhere else in the Far East.

In Shanghai's expanding satellite towns, heavy industry is marching to the east and light industry to the west. The aim, as announced at the time of the 'Great Leap', which became the 'Great Retreat' (1958), was 'a modern industrial base with chemicals, ship-building, textiles, rolled steel plants and a wide range of light-industrial production; quantity and quality levels to surpass British performance by 15 years.' (That time-limit has been quietly dropped.) Can Communism harness, organise and develop Chinese labour as effectively and profitably as colonial capitalism did? It is the old question. And it is still unanswered.

*   *   *

What have the Communists done to life and living in Shanghai? They work in dull, drab, repressive ways their Maoist wonders to perform.

The exclusive monuments to foreign prestige and wealth are at long last being used by the Chinese people who built them and who for decades did not have access to them. The racecourse has become a People's Park; the members' stand is a museum for Communist souvenirs and photographs of Chairman Mao and the late Stalin; the home-turn and the judges' box have been replaced by a winding, willow-hung canal and a bamboo bridge. The hallowed Shanghai Club (Number 3, the Bund) is a seamen's club, with a gymnasium in the smoking-room where the oldest members once slumbered after tiffin in deep armchairs under copies of *The Times*. There are mechanical horses for children, the customary photographs and, outrageously, some sort of pinball machines in the old squash courts — the machines operating of course for skill and clean amusement, and not for gambling profit or loss. The famous Long Bar — 110 feet — has been cut into three sections by party vandals and peddles peanuts and ice cream for children, as well as beer, copies of Chairman Mao's 'thoughts' and badges of the Grand Old Man in profile for foreign seamen, gloomily enduring their tedious shore leave in what was once the lustiest, liveliest port in the Far East.

The Hong Kong and Shanghai Bank has become the headquarters of the Shanghai People's Council. The handsome bronze lions at the entrance had been removed when I was first back in Shanghai, but had mysteriously reappeared when I returned, and their paws were once more being stroked in invocation of health and strength by passers-by as zealously as in the old unenlightened days of Western exploitation. ('Why did you put the lions back?' I asked my guide. 'We are not concerned with superstitious ideas about stone lions or any other capitalist monument,' he replied stiffly. 'Well, then, why take them away in the first place?' More stiffly: 'Doubtless there was a reason.')

There are only dens of virtue and haunts of morality and self-criticism on Shanghai's once lively entertainment front.

Madam Mao's new party-line ideas for Peking Opera are rehearsed in the former Great World amusement centre. Delmonte's fashionable nightclub and gambling-house (operated by the formidable American 'Demon' Hyde until late 1940) is today a school for drama. The exclusive British Country Club has been converted into an athletic training school. (I inquired on my second visit about the fate of the life-size oil of Queen Victoria, which once brooded over the Club's cathedral-like dining-room. It is an interesting revelation of the way the Communist regime operates that, although I got no response to my repeated requests for interviews with individual professors at Shanghai University, who had criticised the party under the 'Hundred Flowers' campaign, I received a prompt and courteous written reply to my semi-frivolous inquiry about the portrait of Queen Victoria: 'It was not listed in the official manifest of Club property; it might have been destroyed by the Japanese army; its whereabouts are the subject of searching investigation'.)

Notorious Blood Alley, behind the Bund, where so many sailors were so often involved in chauvinistic argument, has become a respectable, progressive area of quiet shops and co-operative noodle-stalls. Mrs Tang Fung, sprightly, middle-aged daughter of the former proprietress of the popular Golden Door bar, was operating the 'Safe and Happy' barber shop at the same address; she told me that she was handling 300 permanent waves a month (a forty percent increase over her last five-year plan), and that her daughter earned seventy *yuan* as a factory worker and her son-in-law thirty *yuan* as a pedicab driver (say, US$28 and US$15.20 respectively).

The women were noticeably better dressed, gayer and more attractive than in Peking or Canton or Nanking; some had fur coats and high-heeled shoes; many succeeded in wearing the official blue boiler-maker's uniform with a feminine air. However, we have since heard how the Red Guards reformed this decadence.

On my last visit, in defiance of party orders untamed fortune-tellers were still operating on the zig-zag bridge near Shanghai's old 'secret garden'. One wrinkled, goat-bearded operator claimed, deadpan, that he had once read Mao Tse-tung's palm, and recalled that the Chairman was blessed with unusually long little fingers: 'The tip of each little finger comes above the top joint of his third finger, which means' — as every good Marxist knows — 'that he can rely upon his friends.' The only hot tip he gave me was that I would return soon to Shanghai; I wish the Peking Foreign Office authorities who approve applications for a visit knew this. (My guide-interpreter, a very young and earnest fellow, was properly contemptuous of my interest in the fortune-tellers, but I saw him later furtively checking the length of his fingers.)

There was no prostitution in the new Shanghai of ten years ago, but today, according to reliable recent visitors, there are licensed quarters, strictly for Chinese, on the upper floors of the old Wing On building.

I talked with members of the secret police in, of all places, the former French Club. They were big, heavy, dull fellows, who insisted, vaguely but doggedly, that Americans were smuggling trained spies from Formosa on to lonely Chinese beaches, and parachuting agents and equipment on to lonely Chinese mountain tops. But they also insisted that these intruders represented no real danger, because the broad masses always tracked them down and unmasked them. The US was — and of course still is — represented as Public Enemy Number One. The people's open-air gallery of propaganda pictures, news photographs and illustrated messages, that stretches along a half-mile front of specially illuminated poster-space on Nanking Road, around the old racecourse, concentrates on vilification of the Americans and deification of Chairman Mao. Graphic photographs and scientific description of US germ warfare in Korea and North China are still on exhibition, flanked now by similar pictures of US atrocities and infamy in Vietnam. Photos are also shown of the notorious sign

'Dogs And Chinese Not Admitted', which was allegedly exhibited outside Jessfield Park, but which all Old Shanghai Hands apoplectically contend had as little basis in fact as the Indian rope trick.   True or false, all the Chinese in Shanghai now believe it.

It is clear from all accounts that the Red Guards have stirred up plenty of security trouble in Shanghai today, where the 'cultural' turmoil has brought all party factions out in full vigour and fighting heart.   Untamed Shanghai will always be restless; it is when restlessness becomes unrest that the wise ruler takes note and care.

*   *   *

In a report on Hong Kong, I seem to have written at infernal length about Shanghai.   But these are the twin colonial sisters. This was the Shanghai I knew when it was, so to say, Hong Kong — or was equated with Hong Kong — and that was the Shanghai I saw after it had first trampled on its past, with understandable satisfaction, and was trying to become part of Communist China.

For the great majority of the Chinese people, Shanghai, it seemed to me with memories of the roaring forties, was a far better city physically and economically than it had been before Communism.   This is a denunciation of past misery rather than a tribute to present prosperity.   By Western standards, Shanghai is a drab, sprawling, dark, unattractive, if still fascinating city, dominated by the skyscrapers which the alien capitalists built, and which, at any rate, are not so much of an eyesore as the grotesque metal wedding-cake once known as the Sino-Soviet Friendship building.

There are still abominable slums.   There is still grinding poverty.   There are few modern cars or modern window displays. But, in all fairness, past conditions can be the only criterion. The test must be expectation of food, expectation of work, expectation even of life — not expectation of Western values or Western democratic freedoms, in which only a minority of

Shanghai's or Hong Kong's Chinese would be interested.

Gone today from Shanghai are the battalions of deformed and diseased beggars and the armies of child street-walkers. Gone are the terrible factories of forced child labour. Gone are the hundreds of frozen corpses in Shanghai's back alleys each winter.

Hong Kong, as a colony, has never suffered these extreme hardships.

I like to think that 'Communisation' will pass as smoothly as, but less bloodily than, 'Westernisation' passed, and that Shanghai will one day become a Chinese city. Mud can be used as a pack to enhance feminine beauty. However painful emancipation has been, Hong Kong's dark sister can regain lost charm and escape the worst of the only two worlds which she has so far known.

WEAK SISTER, DYING

Macao, by a pleasant conceit, is not called a colony. Lisbon insists that it is, and has always been, a province and an integral part of Portugal. It is the oldest European settlement in the Far East, a three-mile peninsula at the mouth of the Pearl River on which the Chinese allowed the Portuguese to build a middleman's trading port in 1557 — exactly one year before Elizabeth I succeeded to the throne of England, and 63 years before the *Mayflower* sailed from Southampton . for America.

The Chinese called the place A-Ma-Kao, which means the Bay of A-Ma. A-Ma is the patroness of seafarers, whose temple is still revered in present-day Macao — or Macau, as it is spelled locally. Outside a sandalwood-scented temple to Kun Yam, the Goddess of Mercy, on the eastern side of the peninsula, is a stone table on which the first treaty to be drawn up between the USA and China was signed, in the aftermath of the Opium War, on July 4, 1844.

Macao is a unique racial and cultural blend of the South

China Coast and the Mediterranean, a wedge-shaped maze of streets, terraces and courtyards, slums, convents, gambling casinos and Iberian villas. No international airlines or world tourist shipping services call. It is approached by ferry-steamer or hydrofoil from Hong Kong (40 miles to the east) and by bus and ferry from Canton (65 miles to the north).

'Macao is put together of very fine buildings, and is rich by reason of the commerce and traffic that go there by night and day,' wrote the Rev. Father Cardim at the Jesuit Seminary in Macao in 1640. 'It has noble and honourable citizens. It is held in great renown throughout the whole Orient, inasmuch as it is the store of all those goods of gold, silver, silks, pearls and other jewels, and all manner of drugs, spices and perfumes from China, Japan, Tonkin, Cochin China, Cambodia and Macassar. Above all, it is the head of Christendom in the East.'

Over the centuries, Macao endured war and revolution, attack from the sea and the mainland, fire and earthquakes. It has survived because of Portugal's avoidance of war with China since the mid-sixteenth century. It side-stepped involvement with opium smuggling. It even escaped Japanese occupation during the Pacific War, which most people believed had signed and sealed the settlement's death warrant. During the late thirties, Macao was a meeting-place between Chinese and Japanese agents seeking a way out for Tokyo from the suicidal Chinese 'incident'.

For 400 years the Portuguese in Macao put their faith in neutrality at all costs. In the December 1966 showdown, when China for the first time exported Red Guard revolution, they put their faith in appeasement. They had floated along precariously on the waters of neutrality for four centuries. They were sunk by appeasement. After the Communist 'liberation' of China in 1949, and until the close of 1966, Macao, a fascinating anachronism, a gay pastel cameo, had subsisted comfortably and happily on tourism and gambling (including the grand old Oriental sport of dog-racing, with faithful greyhounds imported from Australia), fishing, the mysterious gold traffic, and small industries such as the manufacture of fire-crackers, matches and incense. The population of more than 250,000 (including 1,200 voting Portuguese) lived peacefully and tolerantly enough under two flags in two worlds which had merged happily.

Unlike the Sassoon skyline of Shanghai, the unique Macao profile is a heterogeneous but harmonious silhouette of Eastern and Western contrasts. From right to left, as the ferry from Hong Kong slips past, are the lofty masts of a Portuguese radio-transmitting station, the Giua lighthouse, the ancient Monte fort with its black cannon and morning-glories, the lichened facade of the ruined Church of Sao Paulo, the grey hulk of the old skyscraper Central Hotel, the white steeple of the Church of Our Lady of Penha, the pink residence of the Governor, the green pavilion behind the two mansions which house the numerous family of the late gambling king, Fu Tak-yam, and the Union Jack atop the British consulate, on the Praya Grande waterfront crescent with its venerable banyan trees.

It is too far from the ferry to see the Communist Party headquarters (near the cobbled Street of Eternal Happiness), the Communist schools, the Communist bookstores, and the Almeida Ribeiro branch of the Shing Hing Bank, the strangest bank in the world and the headquarters of the Macao gold syndicate. But those invisible landmarks were — and are — the centres of real power in Macao. Until the December 1966 showdown, they ruled by Oriental indirection. Since then their authority has become nakedly Chinese and Communist.

Riots and terrorism, destruction and looting, an avalanche of Chairman Mao's 'thoughts', a blight of anti-imperialist posters, and a pandemonium of loud-speaker threats reduced the Portuguese authorities to capitulation. Every concession encouraged a further demand, from punishment of policemen to compensation for law-breakers, from the termination of sanctuary for Chinese escapees to the handing over of bound

Chinese Nationalists. 'Had China demanded that the Governor be guillotined,' as one foreign commentator wrote, 'Portugal would have delivered his head on a salver.' Like the Germans and the Japanese, the Chinese, it has been well noted, always show their worse traits when they are winning and their worst after they have won.

It is now known that when the Red Guard arrogance reached top amperage, the unhappy Governor at last jibbed at one final humiliation, shrugged and demanded one month's grace for the Portuguese to evacuate Macao, taking with them only personal possessions. For the first time the Chinese bullyboys, serving their Canton masters, paused and brooded. But while they brooded, Lisbon urgently demanded a withdrawal of the ultimatum and humble acquiescence. That was the end. Macao passed openly under Chinese control, although the Portuguese flag still flaps in the east wind.

Obviously the Chinese Communists do not yet wish to kick the Portuguese out and absorb Macao physically as they absorbed Shanghai. They wanted to smear the Portuguese flag but not to haul it down. The implications for Hong Kong are clear.

Other observations are of significant interest to Hong Kong. Comrade Ho Yin, the long-time front man for the party in Macao, the chairman of the Chinese Chamber of Commerce, the man who once ran the gambling concession in partnership with the late Fu Tuk-yám, the boss of the gold syndicate, and an honourable member of the National People's Congress (China's rubber-stamp 'parliament'), did not approve of the Red Guard tactics. The Chinese, undercover, were running and milking Macao. What advantage was there in beating gongs, painting Chairman Mao's thoughts on the banyan trees, defacing the beautiful Sao Paolo ruin, bellowing abuse through megaphones? The only direct results would be the frightening away of tourist visitors and trade, and a serious threat to the gold racket.

(Comrade Ho Yin's own bourgeois style of life might also

be vulnerable to censure, his limousines, his luxurious villa and his nights out at the dog-races — the last interrupted by a grenade tossed at his party by a miscreant with some sordid capitalist grievance from a lavatory window in the grandstand, injuring one of the innocent ladies in the Ho Yin party.)

An interesting reflection is that, although they outrage all Chairman Mao's simon-pure ideals, nothing has been done in Macao to interfere with the gambling casinos or the gold traffic. The Augean stables of the Chinese Nationalists in the city-province were cleansed. But public gaming for private profit and a capitalist racket with world connections have been protected and preserved. The latter enterprise merits examination.

The headquarters of the world's biggest gold syndicate is located in a dirty, single-fronted building, with steel grille-doors and an armed guard, at number 175, at the eastern end of the arcaded Avenida Almeida Ribeiro. This is a branch of the Shing Hing Bank, which discourages banking business.

Once I squeezed my way through the grille-doors, crossed the tiled foyer into a shuttered banking chamber, and told a Eurasian with a green eyeshade at the bare counter that I wished to open a banking account. He regarded me first with astonishment, then with suspicion. 'There are other banks,' he said, adding with magnificent understatement, 'Only money-changing here.' He was joined by a stout watchful Chinese in high-collared gown, and they both silently bowed towards me as I squeezed my way out again into the street.

The plain fact is that, year after year, a fortune in gold bullion passes through that narrow door of the Shing Hing Bank — averaging from forty to fifty million US dollars annually. The bullion comes openly and legally from all parts of the world to Hong Kong, whence it is transported — formerly by sealed seaplane, now by ferry — to Macao, again openly and legally. Portugal does not belong to the International Monetary Fund and accordingly is not subject to the Fund's regulations on the import of gold. So whoever wants to ship gold to Macao can do so — and does so, with the perfectly legitimate assistance on commission of Establishment firms in Hong Kong.

What happens afterwards is private and presumably, alas, illegal. It may be that the bullion remains profitlessly in a deep dark hole under the foundations of the Shing Hing Bank as an improbable Portuguese Fort Knox in impoverished Macao. But all the evidence supports the conviction that the bullion is melted down on the premises from the international 27 lb gold block into nine-ounce gold bars or doughnut-shaped oblongs, which are handy to carry or secrete, and which are then smuggled through or around Hong Kong to illicit gold buyers in South East Asia, India and Latin America.

The Macao Government officially collects 42 cents an ounce on all gold imports; this is the basis of the colony's straitened economy. It knows nothing, officially, of gold exports. Nor, it appears, do the directors of the syndicate which buys the monopoly of the gold traffic. Comrade Ho Yin, with his Peking affiliations, assumed control of the syndicate on the recent death of his illustrious partner, the late Dr Pedro Jose Lobo, who was reputedly worth £10 million.

I once lunched with Dr Lobo, a thin, prim-looking Portuguese born in Timor and then in his early seventies, at his home, in the company of Ian Fleming, who fenced with him adroitly over details of the gold business. I append Fleming's record of the conversation ('Thrilling Cities'), which may now be of more immediate interest to Peking and the Bank of China:

Was I correct in thinking that Dr Lobo bought gold from, say, the Bank of England at thirty-five dollars an ounce, and then sold it at a premium to anyone who cared to buy; how it then left Macao for the outside world being none of his business? Yes, agreed Dr Lobo, that was more or less the position. Nowadays the business was difficult. Before, when the premium over the official gold price had been higher, it had been more interesting. Smuggling? Yes, no doubt such a thing did take place. Dr Lobo smiled indulgently. The people in these parts liked to have a small piece of gold. If they bought gold in Macao, I insisted gently, how did they get it out? Dr Lobo's face went blank. These were matters of which he knew little.

The trick, then, is to get the gold out of Macao. It is done in a variety of ways, which Communist supervision and technique in Macao may now seek to improve. It is carried out in hollow bamboos, hammered into thin plates and worn as belts, sewn into mutilated bodies of live fowls and ducks (which at least survive the ferry passage and then can also be sold at cut rates), swallowed by cows, and even 'concealed inside the person of the traveller' (as the court is chastely told). The bulk, of course, goes by junk. There is a jest in dubious taste that anyone can determine the annual value of gold smuggled out of Macao by simply multiplying by four the amount successfully intercepted by Hong Kong's anti-smuggling patrols, that allegedly being reckoned a fair impost on the principal source of income of a sister colony.

The Red Guards made no attempt to suppress gambling when they rampaged through Macao, although their excesses scared away foreign gamblers. If the inflamed xenophobia does not cool down, an expensive programme, costing nearly twenty million US dollars, for a large new tourist hotel, glittering casino, artificial lake, and improved resettlement blocks (in that order), will certainly be unjustified. A Hong Kong-based syndicate, which wrested the gambling concession from Macao interests in 1961, is pledged to complete this developmental scheme.

Normally, US visitors are not supposed to gamble in Macao because some of their lost dollars will find a way to Peking. By all accounts, this ban has not been scrupulously respected.

On-the-spot anti-American sentiment may prove a more powerful deterrent than remote Washington interdiction.

The troubles in Macao have, in fact, revived pressure in Hong Kong for legislation to allow gambling in the colony, where only horse-racing and lotteries (in off-racing season) are now permitted. Greyhound racing, in common with a bastardised form of bull-fighting, flourishes in Macao — or rather, *has* been flourishing — and there is heavy illegal s.p. betting on the Macao dogs in Hong Kong. The rising East Wind might well succeed in blowing dog racing into Hong Kong.

(Greyhound racing in Macao has been burdened by two esoteric Oriental handicaps, which are annoying although strictly non-ideological. The dogs are often temporarily blinded by devoted dog-handlers, who, tempted by bookmakers, smear liquid opium in the eyes of the trusting animals under the pretence of petting them as they go to the starting-post. The other annoyance to dog-trainers has been a tendency by the Chinese kennel-boys to steal, cook and eat the special, vitamin-rich dogs' meat imported from the US.)

No one is quite sure what bid was made by the Hong Kong syndicate of Mr Stanley Ho and Mr Teddy Yip which captured the eight-year gambling concession from the old monopolists, the omnipresent Ho Yin and the late Fu Tak-yam, whose death was hastened by this reverse. Fu had retained the concession for 24 years, making a handsome profit after paying an average of £150,000 to the Portuguese Government in the final years of his rule. He concentrated his gambling in the old Central Hotel (next door to the Shing Hing Bank), which he petulantly closed down when he lost the concession. He maintained three charming wives, a loving family of nine sons and ten daughters, and was an eight-pipe-a-day opium smoker. He had been a bodyguard to warlords in the Canton area in his wayward formative years, and was sharper with the pistol than with the pen. He flew his own personal flag — the golden horns of a water-buffalo rampant in a crimson field — and the Portuguese, with their customary tolerance, encouraged his Chinese individualism, independence and nationalism.

Fu was one of the last old-style Chinese individualists on the China coast. Jardine and Matheson would have understood him better than Mao Tse-tung could. The stories about him have passed into legend. He reputedly shared Sherlock Holmes's weakness for indoor pistol practice at the family residence. According to one story, perhaps apocryphal, he had the hearty habit, in his middle years, when the port was being passed after the ladies had retired, of firing a revolver under the table 'to see who was the lucky man'. In his mellowing years, he disclaimed this story with a thin smile, but it is seriously reported that two of his retainers on the pension list had wooden legs.

Fu was kidnapped in 1946, while smoking opium in a Buddhist retreat, and his family paid £62,500 for his release. When one of his sons was kidnapped in 1953 and a similar ransom was demanded, Fu refused to pay, pointing out with Chinese reasonableness that he had enough sons anyway. His number three wife, who was the mother, was feminine and weak enough at last to secure her son's release for £50,000.

The passing of Dr Lobo was a blow to Macao's tradition of Portuguese financial autonomy and acumen on the China coast; the passing of Fu Tak-yam was a blow to the 'province's' recognition and acceptance of native Chinese talent in another field of commerce. One has the impression that Comrade Ho Yin and the new Communist overlords would have got on more cosily with an ancient, sharp-shooting, illiterate product of the warlord era like Fu than with the young, cool, Western-educated products of contemporary Hong Kong like Stanley Ho and Teddy Yip. True, they are all Chinese, but it is harder for Hong Kong Chinese to come to terms with Communism than for warlord Chinese to do so.

*   *   *

Macao has shown Hong Kong that neutrality is not enough and

that appeasement is suicidal. Macao has been a weak but remarkably durable colonial sister. She knew her station in life and never tried to rise above it. In her harmless, set and declining years, she was tolerated, and allowed to retain her few remaining baubles because they were in pawn anyway to her master. He finally became hectoring, but he did not actually turn her into the street. He took satisfaction in shaming her — needlessly, it would seem — but is still allowing her to pay her board. While it suits him.

As Lawrence Kadoorie, whose family lost all its Shanghai holdings when Communism moved in, and who restored their fortunes in Hong Kong, told the press in 1960: 'The colony's survival depends on its importance to both sides. Macao has lasted for 400 years because somehow it's been useful. If Hong Kong can continue to be useful, it can last as long.'

HALF-SISTER, NUBILE

Singapore, the Lion City, was a British colony. It sprang up from nothing like Hong Kong and Shanghai, but twenty years earlier. It was not raped by an 'unequal treaty' or seduced by opium and contraband. It grew up in mud and marshes like Shanghai. Its founder was another British adventurer, Stamford Raffles, who saw the island as 'an emporium . . . to secure to the British flag the maritime superiority of the Eastern seas'. It passed peacefully from colonialism to *merdeka* (freedom). With goodwill on both sides, it has become an island-city-republic with a population of two million — 75 percent of whom are *hua chiao*, or overseas Chinese.

Singapore cannot therefore be strictly called a sister of Hong Kong. A half-sister, perhaps; a Chinese half-sister.

But the physical resemblances between Singapore and Hong Kong lend the half-sisterly relationship a strong family likeness: the same deep-water port, the same strategic location, the same expedience and hard-working independence, the same lack of resources, the same vulnerability, the same industrial drive, the same teenage Chinese population, the same rising living standards.

Singapore's difficulties, achievements and policies are useful guide-lines for Hong Kong.

The Lion City's biggest asset is Prime Minister Lee Kuanyew — a striking advertisement for post-colonial individualism, although Lee, probably the ablest political leader in Asia, is a Cambridge-educated socialist, whose dominant People's Action Party in pre-*merdeka* days was regarded by the conservatives as pro-Communist. Lee bestrode and bestrides the island, his talent, political acumen, imagination, ruthlessness, restlessness and opportunism frustratingly confined.

Lee and his PAP are still socialists, but they encourage what is called 'guided capitalism', which is a good two-way bet. They are neutralists, but they know that they live in an imperfect world and that neutrality needs defence treaties. British bases, legacy of colonialism, also mean employment. They were in favour of a Federation of Malaysia, which was supposed to unite Singapore, Borneo territories and Malaya in a loving embrace. But the Malaysian patrician leader, Malaya's Tunku (Prince) Abdul Rahman, didn't like Lee, the socialist, or trust Singapore's Chinese. So Singapore was suddenly thrown out of the Federation.

Lee has accepted post-colonial reverses with no wringing of hands, but with cool planning and calculated theatricalism. He is a spell-binding orator in Chinese, English or Malay. He democratically trampled his fatuous Communist-line (Barisan Socialis) parliamentary opposition and put his killer outlaw Communist opposition into prison.

A few Western freedoms have admittedly been bruised in the process. Extremist unions are de-registered, which means that union membership is falling off despite the growth of the labour force under the government's industrial programme. Indeed, an intellectual exercise in Singapore's somewhat *chi-chi* foreign-devil society these days is anxious speculation over the alleged sabotage of academic freedom and liberal disputation because of the iron strength and overwhelming success of Lee's PAP. To the earnest visitor, this twittering denigration of a political leader because of the extent of his success, founded and persisting on free voting, is like a shower of bunkum and horse manure.

Hong Kong is a British island-colony, encompassed by hostile Chinese Communism — and by Chinese nationalism. Singapore is a former British island-colony which has been transformed into a Chinese outpost, encompassed by putatively hostile Malays in Malaysia and Indonesia. Both half-sisters still rely, in any showdown, on the Union Jack.

Although Singapore may soon displace London as the world's fourth busiest port, the former colony has turned to industrialisation as its only hope for survival. Mr Lee will do business with the devil — whatever his politics and race — if that business will bring investment capital to his island-republic. He has the same instincts as Jardine and Matheson, and it is interesting to speculate on what line he would have followed had he been confronted by Imperial High Commissioner Lin Tse-hsu in the Canton *hongs* a century and a half ago. Come to think of it, a Chinese freebooter might have more easily outwitted a Chinese mandarin.

Lee has a great respect for Raffles. 'When he landed here on January 29, 1819,' he recently told a group of visiting British businessmen, 'there were 120 Malays and 30 Chinese [in the mud village called Singapore]. He decided that the future trade of the East India Company would flourish and expand if he used this as a base and attracted the skills of all the people in the region. . . . Within three months, the population had increased to 5,000 Chinese, but there were still only a hundred-odd Malays. . . . We have since created this out of nothingness, from 150 souls in a minor fishing village to the biggest metropolis two degrees north of the Equator. It is the only place so near the

Equator where people do not go to sleep after half-past two if they have had a good lunch. . . . But for Raffles this would still be a mud flat. So we have left his statue outside the Victoria Memorial Hall.'

All Lee's efforts—and here Hong Kong could with advantage begin already to copy him — are directed towards finding better jobs and improving living conditions and opportunities for the younger generation: half the population is under seventeen years of age. He is training what he calls a 'Rugged Society' — multi-racial, multi-religious, multi-cultural. Under a two-year pro-gramme of national service, he is drafting Singapore's nineteen-year-olds into integrated camps of Chinese, Malays and Indians for military and industrial training, the learning of another language, and the fostering of a national Singapore identity — a blend of Israel, communes, labour camps and Baden-Powell. He has always sought to integrate the island's mixed population: a citizen of Singapore must be neither a Chinese nor a Malay nor an Indian, but a Singaporean.

Singapore has first-class housing, family planning and education programmes. The Government hopes to have built 100,000 apartment units by 1970. Exports are up 10 percent over 1966. Manufacturing output increased by 16.6 percent, employment in industry by 13.8 percent (to 48,000), and pioneer investment firms have grown from 100 in 1964 to 113. Per capita annual income is US$533, one of the highest in Asia. Per capita value of external trade is US$1,293, one of the highest in the world.

Yet such is the population pressure that employment prospects are gloomy, domestic exports must increase by an average of thirty percent over the next three years, and the British are resolved to cut back their bases and so reduce em-ployment.

Lee remains confident. 'We are still buccaneers in a small way,' he has said. 'We started off as buccaneers, and not altogether unsuccessfully, because otherwise we would not be here.   We have a very keen sense of property.   We want more property.'   (Strange talk for a Cambridge-educated Chinese socialist.)   'The British and the Chinese, I think, have a certain affinity of soul.   There was a reason why we came together in Singapore.   The kind of ventures on which we are going to embark means that we must be fairly confident of each other for at least one or two decades.'

For his part, Lee is offering the British industrial priorities at withering British bases, so that surplus labour and redundant equipment can be switched to shipbuilding, civil aeroplane maintenance and low-priced manufacturing generally.   The Singapore logic is that when the British pull out — 1975, most think, at the latest — there must be collective regional associations between the non-Communist states of South East Asia. Otherwise there will be economic collapse, subversion and internal aggression.   Australia's Asian destiny grows nearer and clearer.

An involuntary tribute to Singapore's financial reputation, despite market doubts and difficulties, was the immediate presumption, following the issue in June 1967 of separate currencies for Singapore and Malaysia, that the Singapore dollar would automatically become of higher value than the Malaysian dollar.   Both dollars are of equal value (three to the US dollar) and they are still interchangeable, but the issue of Singapore currency is legally and strictly bound to the value of foreign reserves and gold; in Malaysia, there is provision for parliamentary 'modification of the percentage backing'.

Merdeka Singapore radiates a mellow, nostalgic afterglow of colonialism: green parkland suburbs, cricket on the *padang* outside the city hall, elegant classical buildings, the Anglican cathedral, slowly whirring roof-fans in Raffles Hotel, the Gordon Grill at the Goodwood, the wealthy *Straits Times* (with the only substantial English-language circulation in the Far East — over 150,000), Dutch *rostaffel* at the Cockpit every Sunday, with a string-band playing the *Blue Danube*.   Singapore has achieved transition from colonialism to sovereignty, from a governor to a president, with urbanity and none of the ugly shocks, vicious repression, dehumanisation of women, and drab 'levelling-down' in which Communism sourly rejoices.

The 'Rugged Society' has found time to flood-light street fountains, and encourages the island's orchids, frangipani, gladioli and flame trees to flourish like *merdeka*. Historic buildings are preserved. The huge, glaring, blaring Great World amusement park is thronged every night. Singapore works hard and plays hard. Here, again, the resemblance between the half-sisters continues, although Singapore has been emancipated from colonialism and Hong Kong is still in thrall. But Singapore leads Hong Kong in dedicated concentration on the new generation which must grow up with a feeling of pride and personal identification as Singapore citizens if the island-state is to survive. Hong Kong has not yet properly begun to work at this.

At a recent Radio Hong Kong forum of Chinese University students, the speaker who won the loudest and most spontaneous applause was the one who, in response to a question about his hopes for the future, replied: 'That China stops being Communist, and Hong Kong starts being like Singapore'.

THE GREAT EXODUS

What other weapons could Peking, in its present militant mood, use against Hong Kong, save direct military takeover (still unlikely) and nuisance strikes and nationalist-cultural appeal to discontented youth (most likely)?

There could of course be a good, honest, bluff approach to London: We must sit down together, discuss and end or revise the 'unequal treaty', the intolerable continuance of colonial rule over Hong Kong, and the lease of the New Territories. This could be a disarming and embarrassing approach to a British socialist government. But it would come more plausibly from a China in the United Nations than from Maoist China in its current bellicose mood. Anyway, it would probably be rejected. Or the British — for the time being, anyway — could safely turn the tables, as with Spain over Gibraltar, by suggesting a plebiscite to discover the real wishes of the Hong Kong people over Chinese or colonial rule.

Another embarrassing approach could be revival of Peking's request for diplomatic representation in Hong Kong, as a sort of Communist counterpart for Britain's consular presence, now apparently ended, in Shanghai. This sounds reasonable enough, but, as already indicated, would mean simply the arrival of a second and rival governor in the colony. No arrangement could be more admirably calculated to stoke nationalistic fires and foment ideological disorder. The British have tried to forget that the original request was ever made. Pressed again, they would almost certainly reject the proposal. But it would be awkward.

Then — horrible to recall — there might be a repetition of the Great Exodus of 1962 (Year of the Hungry Tiger). This is a sweating memory that can still make any Establishment man in the Hong Kong Club mop an ashen face with trembling hand and call for a double pink gin. There have been many theories about this Chinese mystery but never an official explanation, although the 'cultural' revolutionaries in Peking have recently tried to use the affair as another stick to beat the disgraced Tao Chu, once strong-arm party boss in south-central China. They say that Tao Chu craftily provoked the unarmed invasion to embarrass Mao Tse-tung. Maybe he did. But whoever organised it — if any one person ever did — succeeded not only in embarrassing but also scaring the living daylights out of Hong Kong. The haunting memory lingers. What happened once could happen again. Like all good mysteries, the story bears repetition. I report it as an eye-witness.

April of 1962 was drawing to a close. It had been a rather uneventful month; the main topics of conversation were textile sales and the usual drought. Then, as May began, Hong Kong was catapulted into world headlines. An unprecedented mass exodus from southern China into Hong Kong had begun.

This mysterious, agonising exodus was to last approximately twenty-five days. Some 70,000 men, women and children, in groups which grew into waves, swept across the seventeen-mile frontier into the port's outlying areas. The Hong Kong Wall or Bamboo Curtain was tested for the first time. But the refugees were permitted by their keepers to break and cross the Wall into the colony. And when the Hong Kong police and military began turning them back, the Communist authorities accepted the distracted refugees with the same indifference with which they had first allowed, and then encouraged, them to flee.

A proportion of the 70,000 made several crossings, coming back doggedly time after time. Perhaps as many as one out of five managed to pass Hong Kong's thin anti-Red line and reach sanctuary. The exodus was possible only because the Communist guards in effect threw open the frontier. It ceased only because the Communist guards closed the frontier. Obviously a similar flood of refugees can be released whenever, and for whatever reason, the Communist regime is again prepared to open the frontier. It must be realised that normal Communist control of the frontier means the cold-blooded shooting down of any Chinese, man, woman or child, desperate enough to approach the barrier which curves and winds across the seventeen-mile border of fast-flowing river, wooded area, stony mountain and precipitous ravine separating the New Territories from China.

When the Bamboo Curtain was raised, the Communist guards withdrew stolidly to their pillboxes. The gathering columns of refugees began to trample down the slender, twelve-foot high barbed-wire fence, which served to mark rather than defend the frontier. As the exodus waxed and fattened, the Communist guards began to direct groups of refugees to convenient points of entry, and to warn them away from areas where Hong Kong's police, augmented at times by soldiers, were massed most strongly. But they did not reject — or apparently resent — the mass return, first by truck-load and then by train-load, of the refugees, who, held briefly and fed by sympathetic Hong Kong police, found themselves back in the homeland which they had sought to flee.

For nearly one month, these thousands of desperate and hungry people were massed along the frontier. Briefly but vividly, those who entered Hong Kong brought with them an authentic and desolate picture of a grey barren landscape of hardship and scarcity, of failing food and dwindling hope, of hungry uprooted thousands either conscripted to farm work or wandering in search of greener fields and happier lives.

There had been warnings of the exodus. In Macao, the mainland grapevine had forecast up to four months before that the authorities of China's Kwangtung Province, which borders Hong Kong, were preparing an extensive 'thinning-out' operation, involving the compulsory movement of hundreds of thousands of people in order to ease congestion in the cities and relieve pressure in food-scarce areas. The rumours agreed that old, infirm and disabled 'useless mouths' would be turned loose on Macao and Hong Kong. It was said that 600,000 surplus factory workers and their families would be dispersed to rural communes, because of a shortage of raw materials for workshop plants, and that a simultaneous and systematic removal of more than two million rural workers would be undertaken from food-scarce regions to other areas. Arrivals from Shanghai testified that the teeming population of that great seaport was being similarly 'thinned-out' by one-third — which would mean the removal of more than two million people.

Late in April, the Hong Kong Government announced that the local population of 3.2 million — then rationed to four hours of water a day — was 'too dangerously swollen' to permit the unrestricted reception of illegal migrants. In addition to the 2,000 or so Chinese coming into Hong Kong legally each month, probably another 7,000 had been entering illegally.

But the Communist guards stood back, and the flood of refugees began within a week.

It soon became apparent that the refugees were not all 'useless mouths'. In the first waves came elderly people, but it was not long before able-bodied peasants, young men and women, predominated. Later came young city factory hands and technicians from Canton and other industrial centres. Some had walked in groups for four or five days to reach the border. In the closing stages, others came by train-load from Canton. Some explained that they had tried to cross months before, had been apprehended and punished by prison terms in a labour camp. Now they openly told party cadres at Shum-chun railhead on the Chinese side of the border that they were bound for Hong Kong. The cadres waved them on their way. The groups of refugees increased as they tramped from points north of Canton and west of the seaport of Swatow, passing through villages and infecting others with their hopes of escape.

According to a wide sampling of refugees, the Communist 'thinning-out' process had coincided with a spontaneous mass movement by commune workers who were on the march, in the old traditional Chinese fashion, away from areas where rice was in short supply and would certainly get shorter, to areas where rice might be in better supply. Indeed, the Hong Kong break-through was reminiscent of the massed descents by hungry Chinese on the foreign concessions in Tientsin, Shanghai and Hankow in the old days.

Factory workers in Canton, fearing imminent dispersal to the rural communes, those regimented groupings of collectives in which work is harder and the food ration lower, heard that rail tickets were available to the border. Some refugees said that they 'had heard' that an advertisement had been printed in 'a workers' newspaper', announcing that Chinese could 'visit Hong Kong to see relatives without exit passes'. So the strange story of an open Hong Kong border spread.

A major influence behind the exodus, therefore, was fear

of tomorrow: fear by factory workers, still clinging precariously to city work, of removal to abhorred labour in rural communes — tomorrow; fear by rural workers, hungry but not yet starving, of famine — tomorrow.

There was no truth in early, and wishful, reports that soldiers had joined the exodus. There were unarmed militiamen, but then most Chinese peasants and workers are militiamen of a sort. No high party official or political personality was identified among the refugees. There were plenty of minor cadres and humble, card-carrying party members, and a number of professional men.

Why did the Communists allow part of the refugee tide to flood over the Hong Kong breakwater? The answer could well be another question: why try to stop it? Leave a hard and unpopular task to Hong Kong. Accepted, the refugees would represent, from Peking's point of view, only an unimportant segment of those uprooted by the 'thinning-out' process, wandering in Chinese fashion in search of more food. Rejected, the refugees — and those in China, hearing their story — would not expect sanctuary in Hong Kong in perhaps darker days ahead.

Much was naturally made of the surprising fact that, although hungry and tired on arrival, the refugees were not starving, and most did not show symptoms of serious or advanced physical malnutrition. But approximately twenty percent were suffering from an eye ailment due to vitamin deficiency, and the skin of many — men, women and children — bore a curious, dried, mummy-like appearance from the same cause. The blunted vanguard of the influx also reported that they represented the survival of the fitter, that the weak and under-nourished had lagged behind along the road, and that many had died. Presumably and reasonably, therefore, malnutrition would be more severe among the ones who stayed behind than among those who sturdily embarked on a desperate sally of doubtful and distant adventure.

An intelligent, thirty-year-old factory worker from the

industrial town of Shaokwan in northern Kwangtung gave a simple vivid account of his experiences in flight. This man, who had marked initiative, had to trek five days to the border. He did not realise that so many people were moving towards Hong Kong until he was on the road. But he had been warned before leaving for Hong Kong that he, his wife and two children would be returned from Shaokwan to their home village because his factory was closing down. His family was not starving; he was able to take enough hard rations for his journey. He hoped to make the crossing into Hong Kong somehow, find work and then send food and money to his family. He did not hear the strange news that the Hong Kong border was in fact open until he had been on the road for two days. He fell in with a group which, at first furtive, grew in numbers and confidence as they realised they had the same destination in mind and discovered, slowly, that they could trust one another. The nearer this party, swollen to a couple of score, approached Hong Kong, the emptier they found small Chinese villages, some of which were populated only by women and children.

One received a clear and moving impression of a growing but unplanned exodus, of spontaneous mass flight, of a rare fleeting surge of adventure, hope and excitement. Doubters who had remained behind suddenly and emotionally decided to follow the lead of the more venturesome and to run away from their mud-plastered huts. Why stay behind when you do not own your land? There were hasty farewells with weeping families, last-minute packaging of rice bundles, pledges of food and money from fabulous Hong Kong. So a typical group of refugees, somehow grown to more than a hundred, eventually reached the Hong Kong border near bald Mount Ng Tung-shan, crossed the border, and scattered. Each refugee ran, seeking a hiding-place. Most were found; some were not.

The food ration in Kwangtung, according to refugees' first-hand reports, then averaged around 1,600 and 1,800 calories a day. (The average in the pre-war years of 1931-37 was 2,150 calories, but the population then was of course much lower. United Nations standards reckon 2,300 calories as the minimum food requirement for the Far East.) The Chinese Communist army was — and still is — fed substantially better; city workers drew a higher ration than most peasants and because of higher wages could buy black-market food. Despite transportation difficulties and food hoarding in more fortunate agricultural areas, the party machine had managed to avert famine locally at the price of under-nourishment generally.

It appeared that as socialised and productive units, the communes had shrivelled to bureaucratic husks. Where formerly a full-blown commune had averaged 4,750 households and incorporated a number of villages, and where approximately 550 million of China's rural population had been divided into 24,000-odd communes, at that time (and still today), a 'production team' of twenty to forty households carried out the shrunken routine of a commune.

The refugees agreed that there had been fewer 'self-criticism' meetings in rural areas. The cadres were a hapless and furtive lot, improvising, exhorting and scraping around, under official fire from Peking for shortcomings, not always their fault. and under the scornful derision of the old men of the villages, whose sterling worth and example had been reprovingly if belatedly upheld by the party. Politically, it was clear, the framework of the commune enabled the party to sustain close and unremitting supervision over the commune captives, whose discipline in labour might have been relaxed, but whose liberty and happiness was still harshly confined. The villages, singly, still owned all the land as they did formerly, as a group.

Communism as an ideology had had surprisingly little influence on the refugees. Hungry people cannot eat dogma, but they do not necessarily blame the dogma for the hunger. The prevalent mood at that time seemed to be one of disillusion, hopelessness and passive resistance to eternal, back-breaking *yun-tung* (campaigns) directed often to futile ends, but not one of active political resentment or smouldering popular revolt. The overriding party drive was for increased food production and population dispersal, at the expense of industrialisation and urban expansion; but there were instructive indications of other indirect retreat and adjustments. For instance, birth control was then not openly advocated — nor is it now—but there was an intensive campaign against early marriages. No one admitted that a middle class should or could survive, but devious overtures were being made to encourage intellectuals and 'former capitalists' to cooperate with the regime as an unabsorbed proletariat.

Despite the passage of time, the remarks of some of these refugees still have topical interest.

A CANTON DOCTOR: I ran a clinic at a factory employing 1,600 workers. It is maintained by compulsory contributions of 2 *yuan* (one *yuan* — 2.9 shillings sterling, or US 42.6 cents) from each worker's average monthly pay of 40 *yuan*. Most of my patients were elderly, suffering from oedema (dropsical swelling) and inflammation of the liver, due to malnutrition and sugar deficiency. I attended a class of political discussion for two hours a day, six days a week. I spent three hours of participation in 'free labour', sweeping, gardening and tidying-up the factory premises each day. My average rice ration was seven *liang* (one *liang* — less than 1½ ounces). (A normal rice ration in Hong Kong for servants is fourteen *liang*.) The Government has increased the number of clinics in factories in Canton. Senior cadres increasingly need medical care for insomnia and nervous worry. The army gets special treatment in military hospitals, which are better equipped and have the best doctors. My pay is 100 *yuan* a month.

AN OLD PEASANT: Now they tell the cadres they must listen to us veterans. But it is hard to teach a cat who has been eating stinking fish how to catch fresh fish.

A COPY CLERK AT CANTON'S SUN YAT-SEN UNIVERSITY: We didn't have enough writing paper, so there was not enough work for me to do. Even if they punish me when I am sent back, they will probably only send me to a commune; they would have done that anyway.

A FISHERMAN FROM SWATOW: We know why our skin has become black in the village. It is because the cadres have added a seaweed plant to our diet.

AN EIGHTEEN-YEAR-OLD MEMBER OF THE YOUNG COMMUNIST LEAGUE: You work when the cadres are watching, and steal food when they are not.

* * *

The exodus was a dramatic warning of the mighty convulsions which can suddenly shake China at a time of national famine or distress, governmental confusion or expansion, changing party or administrative policies. All China's neighbours — not only Hong Kong — can be swept by these convulsions. Why did not refugees pour also into fraternal North Vietnam? Or into helpless, wide-open Burma?

Some party Pharoah — perhaps in Canton and not in Peking — let the people go. The British Government was embarrassed by uninformed Western reactions against Hong Kong's refusal to accept refugees from Chinese Communism. Would not Western Germany, it was argued, have accepted a similar flood of East Germans, even if seeded with spies and saboteurs? There had been pathetic scenes when hundreds of Hong Kong Chinese, carrying messages, money and food parcels, approached the temporary camps in which the refugees had been held, calling aloud the names of long-separated friends and relatives who they suspected might have made the dash for Hong Kong.

There were also plenty of ugly incidents when opportunistic Chinese, cashing in on the tragedy, concealed hand-picked escapees in the New Territories while they extorted bribes from anxious relatives in Kowloon and Hong Kong island. After the bribe was paid, the escapee had to be guided or had to thread his own way through an inner line of reluctant guards into Kowloon, where, according to the unwritten law of the colony for all illegal entrants, he was safe once he had reached a central registration office.

Anyway the British Government formally protested to the Chinese Government, and another party Pharoah — certainly this time in Peking and not in Canton — ordered that the tide be dammed and that the Red Army guards and their dogs be re-alerted along the frontier, while the Hong Kong police rebuilt and strengthened the barbed-wire Wall. Overnight the situation was restored to 'normal', and Communist guards were again shooting down any Chinese who sought to cross over.

The exodus accordingly raised many questions but answered few. It had provided a close-up of hardship and discontent in southern China at that time. It could have been one of the earliest warnings that persuaded Chairman Mao to launch his 'cultural revolution' three years later. And, whether so intended or not, it served notice on Hong Kong that the Wall could not hold back engulfing waves of mainland Chinese if Peking elected to release them again. The human waves could return — all the more irresistible because they came unarmed, and because the army could intervene when they were turned back and if their orders, next time, were to press forward.

so what now?

Hong Kong and its four million expatriate Chinese sustain their continuing colonial status because of Chinese consent in Peking. This dependence would be the same were the Peking Chinese now Nationalists, revisionist running-dogs, 'the small handful of persons in authority following the capitalist road', Titoist Communists, or the omniscient Maoist dynasty with its mistrustful party mandarins, managerial eunuchs, and snotnose Red Guards.

That is one of the few hard facts which have emerged from

this fragmentary review of Hong Kong. The riots of May 1967 were the first with which Peking had been directly connected; the first in which the 'backing of 700 million Chinese' was pledged to their persecuted compatriots in the British 'fascist' colony; the first in which the Hong Kong Government was personally insulted; the first in which Chairman Mao's holy name and image were invoked; the first in which impossible 'tremble-and-obey' demands were served by the Peking Government on the UK Government.

Although the demands were never answered and never repeated, and although the demonstrations — at the time of writing — appear to be fizzling out, the events have transformed relations between Peking and Hong Kong. The colonial authorities are proceeding on the prudent assumption that, having learned the lesson of their serious miscalculation, the party agitators are re-considering strategy and trying to strengthen their organisation, extend their influence and rally or intimidate more solid union and worker support for the next ventures. The relatively weak and mainly faceless party movement in Hong Kong is of course infiltrated and the colony's Special Branch manages to keep a delicate finger on the Red pulse. The May 1967 disturbances came as a surprise because of the reckless haste with which newcomers from Canton, reflecting the new pro-Maoist 'cultural' aggression of the reformed provincial committee and the easy triumph in Macao, took over from the Old Brigade in Hong Kong, whose former protectors and allies had been thrown out of office.

Previously Peking's grumbles against Hong Kong had been confined to complaints that the harbour was being used as a US base in the Vietnam war — although Soviet ships, carrying oil and supplies to Haiphong, use the harbour in common with US carriers and navy vessels. There have also been desultory protests against the censorship of Communist films, and charges that Hong Kong is a training camp for Nationalist saboteurs, whom the colony regularly rounds up and deports to Formosa.

Peking's forced and empty nonsense over the Kowloon 'Walled City' has already been noted.

Since May 1967, however, Hong Kong has cast aside illusions and is girding itself to confront sharper and sterner Peking challenges and pressures.   Unless London unaccountably backs down, the colony's opposition to Communist bullying should remain steadfast.   The lines have been drawn — firmly.   There is indeed a cautious feeling that the miscalculated disturbances may have been a well-disguised blessing because of the harm done to the Communist cause among putative supporters and because of the ordeal under fire which the colony's ill-paid policemen survived so well.

Ironically, the notorious 'gap between Government and people in communication and understanding', to which the Commission of Inquiry into the ferry-fare riots in 1966 drew pointed attention, was partly bridged by the common stand against the 1967 violence.   There are pious hopes that this closer contact between an aloof or diffident administration and an isolated community will be strengthened and not allowed to lapse.

The question is whether Hong Kong can learn the lesson quickly enough and make the changes and readjustments necessary for stronger defence as effectively as the enemy is reorganising for stronger attack.

It seems certain that Peking does not propose an armed takeover.   As the crack goes here, Peking could take Hong Kong with a telephone call.   But there would be risks.   There is a garrison of less than 10,000 British troops who would fight and technically start a war, and the Chinese cannot be sure — even if some British have their doubts — that the US Seventh Fleet would not intervene and treat Hong Kong as another anti-Communist, or non-Communist, offshore island.

But there is the new possibility that Peking, under the 'cultural' call to 'put politics in command', is prepared to harass Hong Kong so that confidence will be lost and investment capital withdrawn, and to accept the loss of the Communist stake for the sake of a political victory. This seems to have been the intention in Macao: to humble rather than to seize.

Consider the self-wounds which China has accepted during the 'cultural revolution' — the destruction of art treasures, the vandalism, the loss to production. Profits, higher wages, shorter working hours, and a larger share of commune earnings have been branded as 'economic bribery'. 'Discredit the use of material incentives and condemn personal enjoyment', says the *People's Daily*. At the Canton Trade Fair in May 1967, the party salesmen had to yield to the party propagandist, who bored the intending foreign buyers with lectures and songs. Trade was hurt as politics took command of business.

At the moment, therefore, there is no disposition to believe that Peking will necessarily continue to spare the Hong Kong goose because of the foreign-exchange eggs. But if the British are wise, they will put their minds and energies, and even some of their profits, towards preparations to hold and strengthen the support of the million poorer refugees, who still want no part of Communism, and the coming generation of Hong Kong adolescents, who are not sure what they want.

The specialists agree that there are many ways in which the long-tried Hong Kong partners, Government and Business, can improve the Hong Kong scene and build the Hong Kong defences against any Communist action other than military action. Most of the reforms are necessarily of a long-range nature. Few of them are new or original. Most of them demand some retreat from, or modification of, the basic Hong Kong creed of *laisser-faire*. Adjustments in part are essential for protection of the whole. If Shanghai had made similar adjustments, its fate could have been deferred. Which, after all, is all that Hong Kong can reasonably expect — an indefinite, long-term reprieve, not eternal salvation. The rewards of deferment, anyway, will be worth more than bank profits. On that point, for different reasons, Communism and colonialism can for once be in agreement.

There has certainly been no cutback in government confidence and development, and allegedly no loss of confidence and development by private investors since the new Communist line in the colony. The Government still plans ten-year developmental programmes: the current one, which ends in 1974, runs to £95 million, and includes the giant Plover Cove dam, which will end the colony's water shortage problems. Another stage in the re-housing scheme will be a new five-year plan — now in blueprint, and subject, it is hoped, to reconsideration and expansion — which is scheduled to begin in 1971. In 1968, work on the under-harbour tunnel — four traffic lanes and high enough to accommodate the colony's London-style double-decker buses — will begin, linking Hong Kong island with Kowloon. Estimated cost: HK$221 million. The tunnel will be completed in two years, with flyovers and re-routed traffic lanes at each crowded approach. In keeping with Hong Kong's traditions, this venture will be the largest and most expensive undertaking to have been constructed, and to be owned and operated, by private enterprise.

The landing-strip at Kaitak, which thrusts into the harbour because there is no room on the land, will be extended into deeper water to receive Jumbo jets. (Today Kaitak serves 22 international airlines, which set down and pick up 3,000 passengers a day.)

The present Governor (Sir David Trench) has said: 'If you have massive problems, you must apply massive solutions. And massive solutions are not always the best.' They may admittedly not be the best, but the solutions — or partial solutions — which the colony will have to adopt can hardly avoid becoming massive. There is an unfortunate tendency to think of these solutions chiefly in terms of voting and political parties and constitutional reform and all the mystique and technique of Western democracy.

It is unlikely that Western-style democracy will be a welcome and lasting pearl of great price anywhere in the Far East. European democracy is not for export. Ideas can be adopted and adapted, but fully-fledged constitutions and foreign notions of self-government cannot be carted around and grandly dispensed like Marshall Aid or gifts of home-made jellies and preserves from the squire's lady to a South Vietnam peasant or a Kowloon dockworker. The lingering preference of Hong Kong's Chinese for colonial conditions rather than the Communist way of life is strictly apolitical and strictly self-centred. It needs greater encouragement.

The sentiment is hardly likely to be strengthened or re-vitalised solely by a wider franchise for the Urban Council or even the Legislative Council. Changes of approach rather than changes in voting are needed, although most of the Western and Western-educated reformers in Hong Kong misguidedly keep shouting only for more ballot-boxes. The worst of all possible policies is to offer what purports to be a Western-style concession, but is actually what Chairman Mao calls 'a sugar-coated cannonball' — and to people who don't care for sugar at that. Such was the cynical concession which the Shanghai Municipal Council, under pressure, yielded when it at last accepted the services of Chinese 'advisers', whose advice was never sought and was seen never to have been sought.

Nationalism is the strongest and most aggressive force in Asia today. The Chinese, one keeps repeating, are vengeful nationals first, and confused Marxist-Leninists second. Mao, the nationalist, won power by using Marxism, or his version of Marxism. The Maoist cult is the strongest and sharpest challenge to the Hong Kong system, because it derives basically from nationalism and not really from ideology. Hong Kong can counter it effectively only by a different kind of nationalism: the development of a Hong Kong identity for the Chinese who live in Hong Kong, and who will need greater incentive to continue living there and supporting the system.

MAO VERSUS HONG KONG

Chairman Mao was a nationalist turned peasant revolutionary. He was not the founder of Communism in China. He was a perplexed convert, introduced to Communism by Peking intellectuals.

Personal emotion and Chinese tradition clearly swayed his reasoning far more than he ever admits today. He had been bitterly humiliated by his poverty; a fellow-student, patronising him as the poorest boy in the class (he was fourteen), offered him a job as a servant. He endured an impoverished and unhappy adolescence. He hated his father. He was largely self-taught. He had been painfully conscious of snubs which he suffered from disdainful professors when, 25 years old, he was a humble librarian's assistant at Peking University. He had read deeply all the forbidden, heady, liberal, anti-imperialist books from the West available.

Mao wanted first to be a teacher: a teacher of the peasants, who, he decided at an early age, although ignored by poets, scholars and political soothsayers, represented the only honest lifeblood for a proud and enlightened, restored and unified China. Party history has naturally omitted to record that in bookish adolescence he was dedicated to the institution of a monarchy, with a free and independent judicial system and an adaptation of English laws. Later he flirted with anarchy.

Foreigners to him — as to most thoughtful young Chinese of his time — were barbarians, swindlers, hypocrites and tyrants. Christian missionaries — big-nosed, red-faced, mutton-reeking — were even more despicable because, with their comical wives, they preached to the Chinese people a hypocritical, pseudo-Confucian defence of Western superiority.

Then, in 1918, thanks to Professor Chen Tu-hsiu and the University librarian Li Ta-chao (the two founders of Chinese Communism), Mao discovered the disciplined omniscience of Marx and the overpowering simplicities of Lenin, with their magnetic appeal — still — to so many frustrated young idealists. Here, at last, was a plan for *action*. True, revisions would be needed to suit Chinese conditions; but apparently he did not begin to realise this until 1924, when, with the death of Sun Yat-sen, control of the Kuomintang passed to Chiang Kai-shek.

In origin, the Kuomintang was as revolutionary as the Communist Party, and Mao, like many others, was a member of both. But for Chiang, the duties which the peasants owed the Kuomintang were 'to provide us with information concerning the enemy, food and comforts in our encampments, and soldiers for our armies'. He never recognised — as Mao did from the start — any duties which the Kuomintang might owe the peasants. In Moscow Stalin continued to 'prohibit' agrarian reform in China.

In 1927, when the Chinese Communist Party was broken and dispersed — when Chiang Kai-shek was brain-washed by the Soongs, and when capitalist Shanghai was given an unexpected fresh lease of life — Comrade Manabendra Nath Roy, one of Stalin's emissaries to China, denounced Mao, the champion of the peasants, as 'completely unstable, one of those who persistently and deliberately sabotaged all our revolutionary plans'. Mao was disgraced and driven out of the Chinese Politburo and the Central Committee precisely because of the initial failure of his disobedient attempts to arouse rebellion among the peasants.

Unshaken and undismayed, he persisted in his view that the heart of successful revolution in China was the peasantry. He eventually triumphed and forced the nominal leaders of Chinese Communism, obsessed with the Marxist-Leninist tradition of proletarian revolt in the cities, to follow his line as the peasants followed him.

Commissar Borodin, Stalin's trusted agent, weeping despairingly on Hankow railway station as he retreated to Moscow, symbolised the official party reaction to humiliation and defeat in 1927. Mao, the Chinese, setting up his printing-presses in a Buddhist temple in the mountains of Chingkanshan, using a Buddhist image as a coat-rack, and gathering his tattered, ill-armed but indomitable peasant battalions around him, was only beginning to fight.

All the tremendous subsequent happenings were a triumph for Mao personally, for his aims, his methods, his patience, his correct assessment and skilful use, in diplomacy and war, politics and planning, of Chinese nationalism. 'Go slow at the start and quick at the end,' has always been one of his favourite maxims. He relied on and championed his peasants, and they relied on and followed him. When he summoned the artist Ku Yuan to prepare new designs for party-line door-gods—the ghostly figures which, down the centuries, have been painted, ferocious and protective, on the door-posts of Chinese houses — Ku Yuan asked humbly: 'How shall I draw the faces of the gods?' Mao is supposed to have replied with a shrug: 'Comrade, I do not believe there are any gods. Make them look like peasants.'

Nor did Mao ever lose touch with Chinese youth. His Red Guards may well prove a double-edged weapon, but their devotion to him, now elevated to idolatry, and their mass response to his summons and appeal to them, as Chinese as well as revolutionaries, demolished all speculation that, with advancing years, his influence and appeal might be diminishing. He achieved, and holds, power as a dedicated Chinese revolutionary, deriving his real strength not from Communism but from the irresistible resources of the chained Chinese peasantry, and the continuing support of Chinese youth, and the mighty upsurge of Chinese nationalism. He not only led a Communist revolution in China; he symbolised the convulsive Asian revolt against centuries of Western dominance.

It cannot be pretended that this dynamic force lacks emotional response in Hong Kong, and will not affect the present and future struggle for the allegiance of the young Chinese in the colony: on the one side, Mao's prestige, cult and nationalist precepts; on the other, the bourgeois freedoms and individualist opportunities offered by the modern successors of Jardine, Matheson, Captain Elliot and Lord Palmerston. And it is folly to ignore the obvious chauvinistic satisfaction of many expatriate Chinese, who know and abominate Communism, whenever a national achievement is announced in China, or whenever there is evidence that Mao has discomfited, scored over or embarrassed the foreign devils.

There is no need to labour the point that the prestige and power of Mao — the revolutionary Chinese leader, *not* the Communist leader — must continue to make a strong appeal to susceptible young Chinese, outside as well as inside China. Undoubtedly the teachings of Mao will gain a following in Hong Kong unless strong and intelligent countermeasures are adopted.

Sir Mark Young, a former Governor of Hong Kong, said in 1945 that the British Government was 'ready to take concrete steps in the direction of internal self-government for the colony'. This, of course, was nonsense. Sir Robert Black, another Governor, said in 1964 on the eve of his retirement: 'Her Majesty's Government considers it undesirable that there be any radical or major changes in the present constitutional position of Hong Kong'. This was nearer the mark.

The latest winds blowing out of Whitehall do smell of change and compromise, but they waft — so far — few hints of purpose or realism, and still tend to circulate, like sniffing English foxhounds, around the legs of a ballot-table.

This treatise is not attempting any learned discussion of the possibilities and advantages of building a happier and stabler Hong Kong by, say, widening the duties and membership of the colony's Urban Council. But the new technical debate on whether more district councils should be created, and whether a universal franchise would mean more effective control of garbage-collection and tree-growing and spitting in the street, does appear to be as marginal and superficial as the eternal Hong Kong arguments about the differences between Hong Kong 'independence' and Hong Kong 'self-government' and how or why one would irritate China more or less than the other.

This is not meant to denigrate any move — even a nebulous franchise extension in which few Hong Kong Chinese show any passionate interest — that would give a minority of intelligent Chinese a more tangible feeling of personal involvement with, and sharing of, Hong Kong affairs, problems and future. But surely the central task in Hong Kong is to win and hold the support of young Hong Kong, of the student, the child, the restless youth seeking a job and wondering, subconsciously, whether the fact that Hong Kong was good enough for his parents necessarily means that Hong Kong is good enough for him.

HONG KONG VERSUS MAO

Education in Hong Kong, bluntly, is not good enough. Of course there has been some achievement, as there has been in everything Hong Kong has undertaken. It is said that one new school of sorts opens every five days. Once again figures are necessary. In the 1966-67 academic year there were 2,300 schools, of which more than 1,500 were private schools; and more than 980,000 pupils, of whom 471,000 attended the private schools. The increase in the number of private schools with a leftist bias and politically-minded teachers has troubled the Special Branch. Students from these schools were drafted for organised demonstrations, and were told to plant bombs and insult magistrates.

There is no totally free education system in Hong Kong. Approximately 150,000 children do not receive even primary education; there is not enough room or space, it is said, which means that there is not enough cash. Opportunities for higher forms of education are even more limited. The provision of subsidised schools to ensure primary education for every child is tentatively scheduled for 1971. A bold offensive to hasten that distant deadline would appear to be an essential reform.

Much more, industrialists agree, must also be done for technical training. There is a shortage of skilled labour, combined with a shortage of technically qualified staff. According to the 1966 census, of the labour force of 30,500 in engineering, professional technologists totalled only 610; of the labour force of 140,000 in textiles, there were — incredibly — only 510 qualified technicians; of 129,000 in other branches of manufacturing, only 400; of 283,400 in manufacturing industries in what is called 'the traditional sector' (as opposed to factories in the properly equipped 'modern sector'), there is not a single professional or qualified technologist. These astonishing revelations may well arouse even greater sensations of awe in observers of the Hong Kong miracle, but they are scarcely calculated to sustain confidence in Hong Kong's prospects for continuing success in an increasingly competitive world. The demand for technical training exceeds the vacancies for training by no less than eight to one.

There is urgent need, also, for more vocational training centres. By 1971, it is predicted, Hong Kong will have approximately two million Chinese below the age of nineteen, many of whom will want, and should be able to expect, vocational and technical training. An untrained and dissatisfied labour force of that size will be a liability rather than an asset to a free-trading colony whose success story has been written by its workers, their industry and their skill. Such a young labour force will also be increasingly receptive to anti-government agitation.

These grave deficiencies in education are magnified by lagging development of modern managerial methods and technique. In its larger industries — notably textiles — Hong Kong has installed modern machinery and equipment, encouraged by the absence of any workers' opposition to labour-saving devices. Twenty percent of Hong Kong's managers and working proprietors never went to school.

Such authorities as Professor Stuart Kirby, for seventeen

years Chief of Economics and Political Science at Hong Kong University, have called, long and vainly, for reform of Hong Kong's 'archaic economic structure'. 'We are a modern industrial and trading country,' Professor Kirby has said, 'but we act and think like a backyard sweat-shop. We do not speak the same "technical" language as other modern countries. We are not suitably connected, in non-commercial ways especially, with the others, or properly represented in their international councils. For a unit such as Hong Kong has become in the present-day world, amateurism is not enough — whether it is imported or indigenous. Our archaism is the continued dependence on sheer labour-intensity, on crude labour power in the mass, which is as dead as Karl Marx.'

In common with a few other specialists in the colony, Professor Kirby, long before the current crisis, has been urging measures to help develop a Hong Kong middle class, now largely non-existent, through the promotion of far more students with primary education to secondary and higher education. Until this is done, Hong Kong's industry and commerce will have too few skilled men at the top and too many unskilled at the bottom, with few if any moving up in the empty middle. As the population increases, this is the sort of static society which must deepen and inflame discontent among the younger, leaderless, restless Hong Kong Chinese to whom Mao and the 'real China' is now appealing.

Other new-fangled refinements such as export promotion, market analysis and scientific research are naturally prejudiced by this dead-end policy. A Productivity Council has now been established — twenty members, all appointed by the Governor, of whom ten will represent management, labour, academic and professional interests, and ten will represent government departments. But this new body can hardly be expected to get off the ground effectively or quickly if the essential promotion of a better-educated and better-trained labour force is withheld.

A correlated Hong Kong reform must be improved social

welfare services — representing yet another retreat from *laisser-faire,* but an elementary counter to Communist attrition against the Hong Kong system. The colony's expediture on social welfare is no more than 1.1 percent of the budget — a trifle too Victorian in austerity for the twentieth century, even in the last of the colonies. The indications are that this miserly stipend will be jacked up, but it would be smart to take this action quickly — in a supplementary budget — so that Hong Kong Chinese can see that the colony is not only strong enough to resist an unpopular attack from across the border, but also grateful enough to reward the people who resisted that attack. Significantly, the party agitators and pro-Communist demonstrators made no attack on working conditions or wage scales in Hong Kong. The comrades concentrated — foolishly, it would seem — on politics and ideology, which, as we have seen, have limited attraction in this hard-headed, pay-by-results community. Their fulminations against British 'fascist' atrocities — later confused by denunciation of US imperialism (when so many Hong Kong Chinese wait eagerly for dollars from American sailors and soldiers) and by even less realistic abuse of Soviet revisionism — backfired so forcefully that it is difficult to believe that the new party direction will not learn from its defeat. The only doubt is whether the Hong Kong Establishment, having weathered the first storm, will also learn at least as quickly.

Another complaint by Hong Kong specialists against the colony's 'amateurish' business methods is the absence of proper statistical information. There are no proper records of the national income. Even struggling India and obscurantist Burma provide this information. There may appear to be only a tenuous connection between figures and percentages about business in past years and the prosperity and loyalty of Hong Kong tailors and builders and students in future years; but the link is vital. A variety of foolish excuses have been awkwardly and semi-officially advanced in explanation of this lacuna; in sum, they boil down to the bureaucratic dictum that Hong

Kong didn't need the figures in the past and consequently should not need them in the future. The tough fact is that many speculators and would-be investors — on whose support Hong Kong is completely dependent — want to know how the colony's commerce and industry marches; they will be inclined, particularly after recent events, to equate silence or ignorance with an economic decline. Something is being hushed up. Unavailable records can well mean lost contracts. Chairman Mao surely has a 'thought' somewhere or other in his *Selected Prejudices* about the unwisdom of buying an honourable or dishonourable pig in a capitalist poke.

Apart from the fundamental weakness on the education and social welfare fronts, the colony's defences against the mainland onslaught were revealed to be most inadequate in the Labour Department and labour-relations sector. The new Mao-line tactics were designed to provoke and exploit labour disputes, however negligible and contrived. They did not succeed in May and June 1967, when they mounted their miscalculated offensive over two petty strikes. But those disputes were their chosen excuse for riot and violence. Had the Labour Department had the power — or even the inclination — to intervene at the onset of those disputes, the comrades would have had to manufacture another *casus belli*. Indeed, it must be submitted that the Labour Department should have known in advance of looming trouble in the cement factory and among the artificial flowers, and should have exercised some discreet influence before any break occurred.

The Commissioner of Labour has expressed himself with dangerous lucidity: 'It is not my responsibility to solve disputes. Direct negotiations are the only effective way of tackling industrial problems. I regard myself as the last resort. We do not go into disputes simply because they are disputes but because we are called in. . . . To interfere right from the beginning of negotiations between management and labour would be a negation of unionism and management responsibilities. If we did so, the Department — which means the Government — would have to throw its weight around on wages and so on, and this would be quite alien to Hong Kong.'

Here is the irritable doomed voice of dead Shanghai, speaking from the tomb. The assumption in Hong Kong is that the next offensive by the comrades — better calculated and better prepared — will be concentrated on the next promising labour dispute. If the Labour Department doesn't go out in future to meet and try to resolve a dispute in embryo, the dispute will be inflamed and delivered to the colony in renewed violence. Serious labour disputes are unusual in Hong Kong, where the worker, on piece-work or not, knows all too well that his wages will reflect the company's success with exports. In Hong Kong's dear dead days beyond recall, it may have been possible to permit management and workers to settle their infrequent disputes in colonial isolation. In the lively, perilous days ahead, it will be impossible to expect or permit anything of the sort. Perhaps the new Productivity Council will move decisively into this area.

Some of the Governor's advisers believe also that the Government, regardless of tradition, will have to assume greater responsibility and control over public utilities, where unions are under most active Communist influence. Transportation — privately operated — was most vulnerable to agitators and intimidators in the 1967 'troubles'. The bus, tram and ferry workers are underpaid, by Hong Kong standards, and their working conditions are difficult. (So, for that matter, are the police.) Shareholders in public utilities want profits — a not unfamiliar Hong Kong aspiration — and the uproar over the projected penny increase in first-class ferry fares revealed the hazards of trying to meet rising operation costs from increased charges, however belated.

There have been radical suggestions that the Government should allocate its transportation royalties to help raise wages, and even subsidise or — heretical thought! — nationalise public utilities. The colony's two electricity companies have already been persuaded to accept official control of profits.

One more vital, obvious and overdue reform is birth control. The Hong Kong Government's excellent and comprehensive annual report modestly makes no reference to the governmental share in this controversial work, which is now carried out earnestly but with difficulty by the Hong Kong Family Planning Association. The Association is privately controlled and financed mainly by religious and charitable societies It is having slow but steady success in peddling the Loop to women in the new, crowded re-settlement blocks, as well as the old, crowded tenements and rural and fishing villages. The colony's birth rate has fallen to 24.9 per thousand from a peak of 34.2 in 1962. It is believed that about half of this decrease is due to the non-governmental family planning effort. The personal approach of thirty-one paid social workers from fifty-four clinics wins most response in an industrial resettlement such as Tai Wor Hua, where more than 50,000 people, or 9,000 families, live in twenty eight-storey blocks of apartments, averaging 120 square feet in floor space.

The strongest spur to fecundity, apart from proximity and poverty, is the traditional Chinese demand for sons: mothers with sons are always more responsive to birth control advice than those who have only daughters. The family planning clinics won more than 16,000 converts in 1966 and expect to keep on doing better.

Hong Kong's Problem of People could be more easily controlled with more active and open governmental support. Singapore's record, with vigorous governmental backing, is far ahead. The Loop is still a foreign-devil oddity in Hong Kong, and there is still sensitivity among Chinese wives over its use. With the typically Chinese lack of privacy in the colony's jam-packed apartments and tenements, every one in the neighbourhood soon knows who has aecepted the gadget.

This being Hong Kong, naturally local plastic plants are

now manufacturing the Loop for export. Just as characteristically, Hong Kong manufacturers, in collaboration with Hong
Kong doctors, have devised an ingenious cheaper local variant
called the 'Hong Kong Triangle'. 'Far better than the Loop,'
one plastic manager assured me. 'Ask any Hong Kong doctor.
Ask any Hong Kong wife. We touch nothing which we do
not improve.' It will be interesting to see what happens to the
Pill, when it arrives in Hong Kong.

FINAL QUESTION

Few old hands in Hong Kong, as we have noted, will bet on the
colony's likely life-span. Hong Kong has lived from crisis
to crisis until now — and not only lived but flourished. Perhaps
the colony has become too accustomed to crises to detect the
fatal one when it looms. Colonialism breeds contempt. I
remember the 'inside' Shanghai reaction when I, a young virgin
amid the old hands, said in December 1940 that I was running
out — and fast — back to Australia, because the Japanese would
certainly be in the war by February 1941. (I was ten months
too timid.) Long-resident authorities and specialists were
derisive: 'The Japs have got too much sense. They've grabbed
as much as they can hold, the little yellow bastards. They know
where the real money is. They won't break their own rice-bowl.
They'll keep most of the China loot by negotiation after we've
got rid of Hitler. Never underrate the Japs' commonsense.
They can't beat the Chinese; how the devil do they think they
could beat the Yanks?'

If Hong Kong, incredibly, is allowed to live out its legal
term of colonialism, the world of that thirty-year-distant era
will have been so transformed that Hong Kong's fate and influence will be of even less importance than, in an atomic world,
it is today. The Chinese, in their terribly patient way, will
have remoulded Communism. There will be no ghost city of
rusting skyscrapers, no vacant tenements, no matter where the

trade is going, no matter whether the East Wind is prevailing over the West Wind or the other way about, no matter who has succeeded Chairman Mao or the opium ghosts of Jardine and the British imperialists. Even if capital is progressively and furtively withdrawn on the model of the Belgian retreat from the Congo, China will move into the vacuum. There will always be traffic congestion inside that Hong Kong harbour tunnel.

But we must lower our sights to a nearer and more plausible future. It has been fine and dandy to write so virtuously about the reforms which the Establishment should improvise as a last-ditch stand in defence of the lost cause of colonialism. There is, alas, nothing new and surely little controversial about any of the propositions which have been advanced. But who is going to finance these desirable reforms?

Will wealthy Chinese in Hong Kong voluntarily disgorge or ration some of their profits in the interests of the starry-eyed impatience of Hong Kong's Chinese youth, some of whom already display a tendency to beat up the police, trespass on the turf of the Cricket Club, deface Queen Victoria's statue and stone foreign devils outside St John's Cathedral? To ask a stupid question is to get a rough reply.

How much more money can the Government — with the most astute prescience — safely extract in extremity from its big business partners without sabotaging its *laisser-faire* foundations, without scaring the steady flow of speculative capital, without dimming Hong Kong's economic magnetism? Can the sacrosanct 12½ percent income tax maximum be heroically raised? To twenty percent maybe? By comparison with tax rates elsewhere, such an increase should not be excessive — although Hong Kong, after all, does not hand out pioneer tax privileges.

Anyway, quoting the Financial Secretary, Hong Kong today has cash reserves totalling £80 million and 'a very substantial and growing stock of assets in the public domain which

are both debt-free and revenue-producing' — and which, therefore, could be rewardingly used for government loans in the
colony. So there is enough cash and credit for an immediate
emergency — or for improved social welfare and education,
which could well defer that emergency.

The challenge to Hong Kong is to disprove old Karl Marx
and to demonstrate, to the satisfaction of young Hong Kong,
that the rich are not getting richer while the poor are getting
poorer. In Singapore, that doesn't happen; in Shanghai, it
always happened; in Manila, it is happening with superb abandon;
in Saigon — well, there's uncontrollable war there; in Seoul,
it is not happening; in Japan, bet your life it is not happening;
in Bangkok, well, you must look in the rural *boondooks* rather
than the neon-lit strips for the answer.

The real, final and only question is: how much is Hong Kong
worth? And to whom? It is a good question, especially about a
borrowed place still living on borrowed time. It is the first
question which Jardine and Matheson and Palmerston would
have asked today. It is the question which young Hong Kong
will be asking, although they will not necessarily expect the
answer to be in cold hard cash. It is the question which Chairman Mao must be asking, if far more important questions about
tomorrow are not distracting his ageing mind.

Whatever happens, it is a question which the Chinese will
answer in their own time and their own place and their own way.

BIBLIOGRAPHY

For more—and far better—reading the author recommends:

ON HONG KONG

Foreign Mud, by Maurice Collis (Faber, London, 1946)
The Great Within, by Maurice Collis (Faber, London, 1946)
British Trade and the Opening of China, 1800-42, by Michael Greenberg (Cambridge University Press, 1951)
Hong Kong: The Island Between, by Christopher Rand (Knopf, New York, 1955)
A History of Hong Kong, by G. B. Endacott (Oxford University Press, 1958)
Asia's Bright Balconies, by Colin Simpson (Angus and Robertson, Sydney, 1962)
Hongkong 1966, Report for the year by the Hong Kong Government, 1967
Far East Economic Review, all weekly issues, 1966-67
Hong Kong: A Society in Transition, edited by Ian C. Jarvie and Joseph Agassi (Praeger, New York, 1968)

ON MACAO

Historic Macao, by C. A. Montalto de Jesus (Salesian Printing Press, Macao, 1926)
The Western Pioneers and Their Discovery of Macao, by J. M. Braga (Imprensa Nacional, Macao, 1949)
Prelude to Hongkong, by Austin Coates (Hillary House, New York, 1966)

ON SHANGHAI

Shanghai: City For Sale, by Ernest O. Hauser (the China-American Publishing Company, Shanghai, 1940)

052873